Indomitable Spirit

To connect and communicate: dawnwillock.com
I'd love to hear your thoughts!"

The Glory of Being Ordinary
Book 1
Indomitable Spirit
by Dawn Willock

Vitality N. 1

Publisher: The Ran Network
info@therannetwork.com
https://therannetwork.com

Cover art: Blank Box
Layout design: Simone Chierchini

ISBN: 9798866128150

Imprint: Independently published on Amazon KDP

Dawn Willock

Indomitable Spirit

The Ran Network

Contents

My husband. For having my back in all my shenanigans.
I am yours; you are mine. The end x

Glorious Words,
from Ordinary People,
about *Indomitable Spirit*

Shari Tiegman
Business Coach

This was the book that I needed right now.
It was like wearing a regal robe of comfort. Dawn writes
so magnificently, with the right words in the right tone;
not speaking down but uplifting all the time.
All those self-sanctimonious books, that say absolutely nothing,
but this is magic, Dawn is magic, it was magnificent.
I can't wait to read it again; I liked it that much.
Get this book out there and start writing the next four
because I can't wait for them.
Thank you, thank you, thank you.

~

Heidi Williams
Sales Copywriter

So many grenades of wisdom, insight, and clarity.
Funny, insightful, provocative, raw, vulnerable.
This isn't about speaking truth to power, it's truth to our
own stubbornness, pig-headedness, blindness, and ego
and hits the insightful button a lot.
Made me feel. Reflective, thoughtful, seen, petty, inspired.
So many value bombs, little paragraphs that delight.
Sound bites, and nuggets of wisdom that are
glorious, delightful, resonant.
I loved the kindness and lack of judgement, the got you,
but also the holding you accountable-ness.
It's like I have a little silk-lined velvety pouch full of 'Dawnisms'
that are her own special kind of genius.

Cathy Taylor
Director and Cold Porcelain Hobbyist

Dawn explores the possibility of making peace with yourself,
embracing the similarities, feeling gratitude for the traits
you have inherited, and seeing the positives.
Pushing hard truths until you sit comfortably
in acceptance and forgiveness.
It happened to be an uncomfortable, but uplifting read,
which questioned my previous coping methods, cutting through
the bullshit that is woven around us all.
Fifty pages in, and I had a little cry.
For Dawn, myself and all the others out there.
Dawn's enthusiasm and positive energy are enthralling,
I found myself unable to stop reading, captivated
by such warmth and fervour.

~

Maria Brown
Property Landlady

True and inciteful, an easy-flowing read, written with honesty.
This is the book I would recommend BEFORE
you embark on self-help.

Dom Nichols
Employee at Marks & Spencer

A brutally unflinching, honest, and brave book.
Dawn's chatty style draws you completely in, it feels like
you are sitting down with Dawn, having a coffee.
The conversation challenges you to examine your own life
choices, in a way that is non-threatening but very real.
You can't help, as you read, but think about the
questions being asked.
I thoroughly enjoyed this, especially considering I don't
normally read this genre, but I would recommend it to anyone
looking for something authentic and unique.

~

Sarah Emanuel
Recruitment – HR Specialist

A brilliant blend of self-help through memoir moments,
a book that wouldn't get lost in either genre.
Unapologetic, captivating and honest—it made me sit up
and listen, cry at the honesty of her own personal journey
and also challenge what the f**k I've been doing and why!
It's truly a riveting read that I couldn't put down.
It makes you want to pick it back up and re-read for the nuggets
of wisdom and practical lessons throughout.
Book No 2, please!

Leon Deakin
SEO Specialist

In a sea of motivational books, Indomitable Spirit
goes way beyond the typical.
It's an inspiring journey that actually gets you asking
yourself the right questions. This is the first thing I've read
for years that changed my perspective.
The author is open, genuinely inspiring, and it has helped
me want to do something for the *real* me.

Foreword

Read this book. Read it now. Read it before you bother with any self-help books.

Discover your indomitable spirit.

Take it from me, as Dawn Willock's editor, that she has discovered hers, and she will show you how to find yours.

Working as a ghostwriter or editor is a privilege, not only because an author is placing their trust in me to help them transform their ideas into the best book possible, but because it often involves being entrusted with sensitive information that they've never shared with another living soul.

They give me their hearts, their minds, and their secrets; and in doing this, they bare their bellies and make themselves vulnerable. This is why I could never work for someone I didn't already admire. I need to feel a sense of empathy with them, and they need to feel the same about me.

An intimate working relationship is just as essential for a me and my client as it is for a priest, a lawyer, or a psychiatrist. Sometimes being a ghostwriter and editor feels like all three of those roles combined—and then some—as the author shares their deepest regrets, seeks to justify their life choices, or grapples with the meaning of life. None of that applied to Dawn. Accepting responsibility, yes, but she's too glorious and indomitable for regret and too busy living life authentically and totally to worry about what it all means.

I've had the pleasure of working with a range of wonderful people from *Sunday Times* bestselling authors to people who just wanted to leave something behind for their children. They've all been extraordinary in one way or another. Dawn's no exception, and it's been a great honour to work with her on *Indomitable Spirit*. She is a magnificent force to be reckoned with, truly an indomitable spirit, so if you want to know what one of those is, you've come to the right place. There's no hypocrisy here. She's the real deal.

As we went through this process together—Dawn writing this book her way, fully indulging in the fun of being an author and laying down the words, phrase by phrase, sentence by sentence, intuiting her way to the end, and me giving her the space to express herself freely (I wouldn't have it any other way, and she definitely wouldn't) and trying to edit the content as lightly as possible—I was struck by her writing style.

Every writer is unique, but Dawn has to be one of the bravest, most liberated, and dominating writers I have ever encountered. What do I mean by that? She doesn't care what you or I think of her, her life, her decisions, and certainly not her writing style. Yes, she recognised the importance of using an editor, but as you will discover in the pages of this book, Dawn listens to her belly and believes that it never gets it wrong. If she didn't want to go with an editorial suggestion, whether she agreed with my logic or not didn't come into it. She would go with her heart and her belly.

That said, and she's given me full permission to go to town here with my honesty, I found her writing style very exciting.

On the one hand, it presented me with challenges. I think she is so used to writing posts for social media—she is an excellent copywriter (and that's coming from a professional who worked in advertising for fifteen years)—that the first draft looked like the longest Facebook post in history. *Dawn*, I thought to myself, *if we go with these one-sentence paragraphs, it's going to be difficult for any one idea to stand out, and your book's going to be as thick as the Encyclopaedia Britannica!* Fortunately, she went with my suggestion that we employ a bit more chunking of ideas into paragraphs.

Then there were the tics to deal with. Every writer has these, whether it's the overuse of phrases such as "to be honest" or "as it happens", or exclamation marks and interrobangs (?!). Dawn's favourites are ellipses (…), exclamation marks, and line breaks. I am grateful for them because they demanded closer attention to detail, which I think has made for a better book.

On the other hand, her descriptive language, not only of scenes and situations but also mindset, emotions, thoughts, and feelings, regularly hit the heights. Dawn is not just someone with some innovative ideas that she needs to put in a book. She is an exceptionally eloquent and articulate writer and far more adventurous than this humble editor.

If you are a shrinking violet when it comes to the vernacular, get over it. Dawn has made swearing into an art form, particularly in chapter four, which is aptly named… hmm… I will leave you to find out for yourself. Never let anyone tell you that people only swear to compensate for having a poor vocabulary. I am sure she didn't need to, but the way she swears is awesome!

I was also stunned by how much of Dawn's life and philosophy resonated. Repeatedly, she used analogies to explain things in a way that I had thought of but never heard anyone else say. I was constantly prodded and reminded of things that I knew deep down but wasn't acting on. Again, to fully grasp the weight of that remark, you have to understand that I am not new to the growth mindset or stepping out of my comfort zone. I know world-class coaches and therapists and am blessed to have many as friends and some as clients, so it's not as though no one has ever challenged me with a tough question. Dawn is a first-class coach—a natural. It's her God-given superpower. She knows that, owns it, and is dedicated to using it for the good of others.

Collaboration on a book project is such an intimate experience, I can't help being impacted when I'm working so closely with someone else's words, but that has rarely led to me making significant life changes. Dawn's words did, so I want to tell you how this book impacted me.

The first time I spoke to Dawn, the conversation had nothing to do with writing a book. I reached out to her because she was running a martial arts association (and still does), and I needed help setting up a martial arts club. I will spare you the details, but let's just say that what I wanted to do was a bit off the beaten track, and I was looking for someone who believed in my mission.

As an ordinary person, I was going with my heart, following my passion, and striving to do something I had dreamt of for a long time. I knew I had something to offer, but I was also aware that I was up against many barriers to entry into the martial arts industry.

That was ten years ago. I don't remember the details of our conversation, but I remember one thing very clearly—how she made me feel. Dawn convinced me that what I had previously thought wasn't possible was well within my reach.

Neither of us knew back then that we would work together on her book, and our paths didn't cross for many years, but our journey together seemed to be pre-ordained on many levels. We even share the same birthday! We have been connected on social media for a couple of years, and I like the way she conducts discussions, how she cuts through the nonsense in the debates of the day, and her clearly very open-minded attitude to life.

When Dawn asked me to be her editor, I jumped at the chance, but it was because of that chance conversation all those years ago that I knew just how authentic this book would be. I had already experienced, first-hand, how she served ordinary people with permission to be who they wanted to be their way.

Sunday, 24 September 2023

Fast forward a decade. Dawn and I have been working together as author and editor for many months, and today we are finalising this book ready for publishing. During this time, it's not just this book that has been edited. Dawn's words have brought about a huge shift in my perspective.

I grew up in a terraced house in south Liverpool, the second youngest of seven siblings—hand-me-down clothes, shoes worn until they were falling to bits, and a handful of UK family trips. Money was tight, and I'm not complaining, because it taught me that self-respect and validation don't come from being able to afford expensive brand names.

I learned to make the most of things from an early age, and, as an adult, still tend to go for practical instead of desire, and bog-standard rather than luxury. I also struggle to admit publicly how good I am at my job. I have no qualms about celebrating my successes, announcing publishing deals, and admitting how delighted I am to start new projects, but ask me how good I am, and I become a shrinking violet. Dawn has forced me to ask whether I deserve more; whether I said no when I should have said yes.

As a result, I have made several massive life decisions.

I have always loved BMWs. On Friday, I bought one! It's the most expensive car I have ever owned, but I finally have a vehicle that I don't just like but love. I deserve it, and I don't have to justify my decision to buy it for myself in any other way than that, I love it.

In less than a week, I will be standing on stage, delivering a 45-minute comedy set. They're paying me. This is a professional gig. That's all well and good, except... I'M NOT A COMEDIAN! But I am doing it anyway, just because I want to! And I'll nail it.

I wouldn't have bought my car or agreed to do this gig if I had not been working with Dawn.

This next bit is a challenge, and I am forcing myself to say it firstly because I believe it is the right thing to do and also because Dawn will tease me forever if I don't. I have taken risks and worked hard, and I can say that I am one of the UK's top ghostwriters and an accomplished editor.

I think, like many others, I struggle to own my own brilliance. So, here I am, taking the biggest risk and owning my brilliance.

Thank you, Dawn.

Dawn's wisdom has awakened my indomitable spirit. It was always there, but it needed tuning up. It's cliched, but it wasn't firing on all cylinders. Perhaps it's still not, but it's got far more power and direction than it did.

I am an ordinary person, like Dawn, like you, and like everyone else. By embracing who I am totally, and choosing to live fully—taking risks, indulging, and appreciating this literally 'once in a lifetime' opportunity to be a human being on Earth today—I can enjoy the glory of being ordinary. That opens the doors for this ordinary person to do extraordinary things.

Dawn delivers the truth that we all need to hear but are afraid to listen to, but she does it in a way that is palatable—with love, compassion, empathy, and a kick up the backside when necessary. She recently pointed out that I have a 'poor relationship with money', which is what her next book is about. And I can't wait.

In the meantime...

I repeat:

Read this book. Read it now. Read it before you bother with any self-help books.

Discover your indomitable spirit.

Martin Morrison—Ghostwriter and Editor

Preface

September 2022

This is really important, as this turn in fate was the pinnacle point, taking the whole thing from writing a book for myself into a five-year social experiment, birthing the idea of a revolution for ordinary people.

Nick James is the CEO of Expert Empires and holds a huge business event in Wembley twice a year, hosting globally recognised speakers. If you're in business, I highly recommend it! And so, in my mind's eye, it made perfect sense that it'd be a great idea to launch the book at his event, which sounds mad now I say that back to myself. However, without either one of us knowing this at the time, without his faith, this journey wouldn't have had quite the same impact.

It went something like this…
"What's the book called?"
"I don't know."
"What's the book about?"
"I'm not sure. I'm making it up. I've only got the first draft of chapter one"
"…Right…" said Nick, followed by a bit of a silence…

That was at the very beginning. It's now five books, and five years speaking.

The Glory of Being Ordinary is the name of the series of books coming. *Indomitable Spirit* is Book 1.

Fast forward a year…

I'm not always easy to work with. It's a fine balance on a normal project, but this book was about making it up and going with our guts, so when it came to the more serious stuff, like marketing and capturing the message, it became more difficult.

I hadn't set out with a core message—other than 'let's see what pours out'—but of course, trying to translate that into tag lines, etc., wasn't very easy! And if any of you know anything about marketing, you know that it's impossible to just say, 'I'm writing for ordinary people.'

We had a marketing dilemma, struggling, and were trying to fit this into 'something'. But we just couldn't nail it. Like any creative process, you must go through all the wrong sentences to get to the right ones. We were at that point of it becoming painful… with a looming deadline.

This is a private email that was sent. Why include this?

Because I want you to KNOW that this book isn't bullshit. That applying some of its philosophy isn't bullshit. That we don't have to be anything other than ourselves, and then the world becomes restored.

Sent by Dawn, Thursday, 21 September 2023, 8.05 p.m.

'I need to just brain dump…

I wrote the book first & foremost for me. Just to see what happened. I guess this book is for other people like me – who wonder sometimes, what if…

I understand from a marketing point of view, that's not classic. And I know I'm not always right, but I do know one thing for sure – if it doesn't sit right in my belly, it's definitely not right. And there in is the point…

What is the point of the book? To listen to your belly. To trust yourself. To play with life a little. To peek behind the door of possibility.

I want to do this authentically. Honestly, I don't care about what other people do. I won't care of we don't sell a million books – although let's be clear, I intend that…

Of course, it's wise to allocate some respect to marketing structure, especially those which are tried & tested & work.

But I'm pulling the plug on trying to fit my round self into a square. For the WHOLE of my life, whenever anything is THIS painful to find, it's because it's not right.

So. Let's stop. Because nobody is having fun!

It is what it is, so let's let the chips fall, by mixing conventional strategy, without the conventional bullshit. Because – it's compromising my soul, which I can't do.

And if we flop a little, that's okay – it's on me. Except I already know, we're not on a road to flop.

Back to basics.

I wrote this book, because I am fucked off…

First, actually, I want to be an author.

Secondly, I genuinely wanted to see what my heart would produce. I wrote this book for myself, but then wondered, what would happen if I went full 'Author' and 'Speaker', just for the fun of it. And in doing so, who else would find some inspiration to pursue some possibilities in their world?

I wrote it because I'm bored of the regurgitated 'noise' and how so many amazing people out there get swamped & suffocated by it and end up settling for mundane – and then get old, full of regret.

I am irritated that people can't see who the fuck they are and can't feel their own magic.

My genius – and it is a genius – is that oftentimes, I CAN see that – in so many ordinary people.

And I want to spark a fire, so others burn as brightly as I can see they can.

I want the future generations in my family to say – she was a fucker, but by God, she didn't let us hide behind ourselves – that one way or another, she MADE us be everything we could possibly be. I want them to say, she put her money where her mouth was and Didn't. Give. A. Fuck.

I promised myself many years ago not to lose faith in mankind – so to sit back when I can see so many lose faith in themselves is not an option for me. Not on my watch. Not while I have breath.

That might sound dramatic, but there is it. Call it what you like – but if I don't serve this up, I am putting myself on that path of regret. And that's a No from me.

So, let's stop over thinking it all. This is the direction we need to go. Let's say what it is on the tin – and the above is what is it, nothing more, nothing less.

Dawn x'

Introduction

Strong, Brave, and Impossible to Defeat: An Indomitable Spirit

This book is a human experiment, a real-life, real-time 'Fuck it, let's put our money where our mouth is and see what happens' exploration. It begins a five-year planned journey where I will step into unknown territory.

I have no idea what I am doing or what the outcome will be, but I am so very passionate about uplifting the human spirit, I figured, what better way to do it than to put myself in the most vulnerable, uncomfortable, uncertain place I could create, invite you to follow the journey and let me take all the risk, and in doing so, inspire you to peek around the doors of possibilities in your world, and to break you away from some fears that may hold you back from taking action. What better way, than putting your money where your mouth is, to demonstrate that ordinary people can do exactly what they want and create anything they like, without compromising their integrity, just by having the confidence to be true to themselves?

I look around and see so many ordinary people living seemingly lovely lives, but when we scratch beneath the surface, we discover discontented hearts, unfulfilled dreams and wasted souls. Unbelievably beautiful hearts and minds who, just because of feeling too ordinary, accept mundane or second best. I also witness thousands of people who sincerely try and have fires burning in their bellies as they attempt to work their arses off to elevate themselves and improve the opportunities and choices for their families and too often seem to miss the mark. I'm not just talking about money and business but also personal lives.

We can implement morning routines and consume millionaire mindset or successful relationship content. However, people mostly struggle, becoming exhausted, or they give up having hardly begun, and that's if they manage to get past the first hurdles. Others sacrifice family time or don't get the recompense they deserve.

I ask, why is it that some succeed, and others don't? Where are my successes and failures, and what attributes do I have? How did I overcome huge adversity and still create my life?

As ordinary people, we may need to take a small step back and build on the foundations that we already stand on before we can adopt an indomitable enough spirit to conquer the rest. I am an ordinary woman, but I am also an indomitable spirit.

How can an ordinary woman feel so fearless, how did that come to be, and why are some of us so brave while others prefer a safer life? What are the consequences of living a fearless life? What are the consequences for those living with fear?

This book comes from deconstructing and self-discovery, the connection I have with myself and other human beings, my partnership with adversity, and my will to achieve victory against all odds. It considers how I needed to stay true to a promise I made to myself as a very young child, to never lose faith in mankind—a noble and romantic notion but one that I kept to. I also explore how those things have delivered my version of success. I guess as I am now in middle age and observe life more reflectively with my awareness of mortality, I am left with the desire to connect with people differently, as ordinary people doing their best. There is a yearning to inspire us all to enjoy a taste of what it feels like to rise with confidence, unstoppability, and curiosity, and to look at life as an infinite array of possibilities.

Indomitable Spirit is for ordinary people, with whom I'd very much like to have a conversation about having an indomitable spirit sourced from self-belief and self-acceptance. I want to bring some comfort and celebrate how glorious and extraordinary we all are—even when we are ordinary! One of the foundations of an indomitable spirit is validation. I want ordinary people to feel validated. I want ordinary people to feel unstoppable.

What the heck does validation mean?

Validation is the demonstration of truth and value. We see countless examples of falsehood, pictures of people living their 'best' lives, and quotes presenting wisdom from self-proclaimed authorities. We seek vanity metrics such as likes, comments, and other external ways to measure our validity, but, unfortunately, much of it isn't true and doesn't reflect our actual value. Many would say that social media has caused this, but I don't agree. It's just exposed how deeply human beings require acceptance, approval, and external validation. We sit in an era where the harsh vulnerability many exist within has been blasted wide open. If anything, social media fulfils an innate desire we all need to satisfy. We just didn't admit it before; although admitting what we know about ourselves is one thing, but acting on that? Well, that's a whole different level of courage.

There isn't a single human being who doesn't already know in their gut whether they are fulfilled, happy, or have settled for second best. Deep down, in the depth of our bellies, in the pulse of every heartbeat, woven tightly in the fabric of our DNA, we know.

As we fulfil our inner 'Rocky', as we put up fighting guards, learn footwork and head movement to duck and dodge the truth, as our ego claims us in the name of protection, we know. While we learn to find 'reason' and 'why for' to avoid admitting it, we know. We hide, pretending, avoiding, because if we dare step into the arena of Pandora's boxing ring, we might have to take some scary-shit action. It takes bravery to face ourselves, face our fears, and overcome the urge to hold back. Mostly, our beliefs are the main cause of our falling short.

This is a book about self-validation. It's about freedom—a narrative that wants to reach out and touch other people to tell them, 'It's okay to seek truth and hold your value, regardless of what you've been through or your starting point.' The purpose is to cut any shackles that dim the human spirit.

It's not about rejecting all external validation but, instead, not relying on it to feel whole and satisfied, and not needing anything external to make you unbreakable and unstoppable.

It's about winning the trophy of self-belief.

Why am I writing this book?

I could keep it simple and say that I've felt driven to start this book for years, but anyone who knows me would ask why it took me so long because I'm anything but a procrastinator. What was I waiting for? It turns out that when my nemesis died, this was the catalyst for writing my book. How bloody annoying that after fighting her my whole life, I will have to credit her for my most significant project! Interestingly, and surprisingly, this credit has enabled the final stage of my healing. With grace and gratitude, I wouldn't change a single moment of her extraordinary wickedness.

Death is a strange thing, isn't it? Even that of an enemy. Even more so when that enemy was embroiled in your life and defined your love rules, the very person who gave you your first breath but then sought to destroy you if you dared challenge them.

She was too big for death but did it anyway, so I guess it forced me to look at time differently. And it turns out nobody is too big for death. I want to share that lesson the most. We articulate that we don't have forever, something we all know but live as though we don't. Instead, we shield our reality with mundane, average existences; not walking our walk, not dancing our dance.

Why is writing this so important to me?

Deep down, in the depth of my belly, I know this is where my life juice is. For as long as I can remember, I have been told repeatedly to be quieter, to tone it down, and to leave things, but that's not how I am hardwired; in the pulse of every heartbeat, I know I won't feel fulfilled unless I write this book. I won't be awarded my trophy of self. I am a communicator, so here I am, communicating.

Woven tightly in the fabric of my DNA, I know.

I also know I see plenty of hopelessness. There are too many unfulfilled people who, maybe, if they read a book that inspired them to be brave enough to admit what they know, could find the courage to be who they are. My sentences could make a difference, making every fracture to my heart, war-torn battle scar, and criticism that has tried to chip me away worth it. I guess it comes down to the love of humankind, refusal to lose faith, and love of self because we certainly can't always rely on others for that.

This story isn't my story but rather, words about the wonder of adversity, resilience, self-worth, and the courage to love. It is about the critical relationships in our lives and how beliefs impact every decision we make, and it dares to challenge beliefs and break down barriers. It's my journey, but it's also everyone else's. We all have the same availability for life lessons. We all get the same opportunity to extract what's in our souls. We are all just ordinary people. The irony is how unimportant a single person's journey really is, and the insignificance of the details, because we live, we die, and the next generation moves forwards. Rinse and repeat.

I could easily apply self-sabotage and decide there's no point in writing my book. There's a chance that nobody will care to read it, and I'll probably piss off people within my circle who'd rather I restrain myself in the box of privacy. But that's not me; I am a gladiator, a warrior, and a shapeshifter, and I am unstoppable and unbreakable, despite what life has thrown my way.

And therein is the point.

I don't want to be quiet. Whether anyone wants to read this or not, I want to sing from the hilltop. It simply makes me marvellously happy. It sounds like I'm disregarding some boundaries. Yes, I probably am, but when I die, I will have honoured my heart, I will be satisfied that I was true to my desire, and I won't have settled for mediocrity. I will have been true and validated myself for no other reason than that it was the right thing for me.

Selfish? Seemingly but not really. It's probably more selfish to stay in the safe lane hoping that everyone will approve of us, to remain dissatisfied, become resentful and, at worst, bitter, and then die knowing our life was unfulfilled. Living this way for too long makes us miserable, and then we make everyone around us feel miserable. Fulfilled people are wonderful to be around, so I choose that. If I seek any external validation, it will be because I am a happy, fulfilled soul.

You'd be forgiven for assuming I should write for other women, but that isn't the point. First and foremost, I'm writing for myself. I am just an ordinary person, and it's always wise to talk about what you know, so this book is simply for other ordinary people—and to breathe some life into how extraordinarily glorious we are.

When you have discovered your worth and find validation from within, gender, age, religion, class, and all those other aspects are irrelevant in most situations, or they should be. I have reasonably strong views on preserving masculinity and femininity. I strongly believe in celebrating all stages of age and the value contributed, as with traditions and different upbringings, but those aspects also shouldn't be blamed for restraining us.

My intention for anyone who reads this is to know you are not alone, so it would be my honour to hold your hand a little. If you've picked up this book, something deep down is prodding you to remind yourself that you know there is more for you, that maybe you're bigger than you dare to admit—perhaps you've settled just a little bit?

Society's current notion of success often translates into the idea that you must be uber-rich or famous. No wonder success is scary for people if that's the only measure because most people are happy with a level of financial security that affords some pleasant choices without any need to sell their souls or forfeit their chance to find fulfilment and satisfaction.

So here I am, publicly walking my walk, talking my talk, with zero evidence of any inevitable outcome. I am writing my book, making it up word by word, sentence by sentence, and I have already committed to speaking on a large stage in a few months—and I haven't even finished the first chapter! I could become a world-famous author and a motivational speaker or fall flat on my face and make a fool of myself on the stage—or anything in between. Let's see, shall we?!

In the meantime, if I do nothing more than fill my heart with joy by writing and inspiring even just a few people to ask themselves some questions, that'll do, and it will have been a success. However, whatever happens to me through this experiment, I promise that you can have it all, with integrity, even as an ordinary person. All you need to do is be a little bit brave, or at least be open to that possibility.

Will you join me in my little human experiment? Are you ready to validate yourself and find your glory? Are you ready for nothing to hold you back?

CHAPTER ONE
Twenty-Four Hours

11 p.m., Tuesday, 21 December 2021

The phone rang. For my sister to call, it could only be about Mom, who was seriously ill in hospital. She was straight to the point: 'They've called Dad into the hospital to say goodbye to her.'

'Right. I'll get there,' I responded, almost matter-of-factly and without hesitation.

'No,' she cut in, 'There's nothing you can do, and they won't let you in. You're not to go…'

I knew my place; I knew I wasn't wanted or welcomed. I also knew Dad would be uncomfortable. He'd see me as causing trouble. One way or another, Mom would also give him a tongue-lashing. His dedication to pleasing her and avoiding getting into trouble with her may have been fruitless, but if nothing else, his perseverance was admirable.

Dad's one of the nicest people I know. His example laid my foundations of integrity, work ethos and appreciation for the simple things in life and how these values could be combined to provide a comfortable life. He set the standard. But we all have weaknesses, and his biggest was Mom and his tendency to facilitate her outrageous behaviour. He wanted a quiet, happy life, but he didn't get one. Would it have made a difference if he'd put his foot down with her?

Probably not.

She was a force to be reckoned with, and her ability to conquer and destroy was magnificent. We all understood the rules; if you challenged her, it would cost you him. He chose to stand by her no matter what she did, which was his burden, but I also had a part to play.

When I was young, he tried standing up to her but lost every battle and eventually lost the war, caving in and choosing her entirely. My behaviour often made matters worse. When you have no protection from either parent, it feels like a deal-breaker, you have nothing to lose, and I did a marvellous job at rebelling. Choosing Mom must have felt like the easier option for my poor dad.

I always knew how things would play out with my younger sister, so there was no love to lose. Her primary drivers were her inheritance, protecting her status and keeping a big sister out of the way. It was all very predictable. She had to do what she had to do to defend her position, and she would protect it at all costs.

It's been an easy win for her because I have never fought for it. She's welcome to it all, and I feel sorry for her insecurities. Mom and I are more than a match for most, so there probably wasn't much space left for my sister. Mom and I stole the show and sucked all the oxygen, so for that, I'm sorry. My sister is just surviving, so I guess she's done her best with a simple strategy—head down, play the long game, and take the treasure pot. Being ostracised wasn't an option for her. Naturally, I became collateral damage.

Would it have made any difference if she had realised it would cost her everything else—health, happiness, relationships, wholeness, and self-worth? Would it have made a difference if she knew the total cost of selling her soul?

Probably not.

Am I a troublemaker? Yes, I guess so. Not appeasing a narcissist will always cause trouble. I chose to go toe to toe with my mother, not to play by her narcissistic rules, and to call out those who indulged her. The backlash from those challenges was not for the faint-hearted, but that's okay—I'm not faint-hearted. If demanding truth is trouble, then, yes, I will wear that as a badge of honour.

I called my daughter, and she didn't hesitate to tell me what she thought. 'Please go and see her,' she implored me, 'Please. Just get in your car and go!' I needed another perspective, so I called my aunt, my wonderful, loving, honest aunt, Mom's sister, and complete opposite—my rock, my salvation, and my guide. Even though she lives thousands of miles away, she's my go-to person. True to form, she brought the issue back to what was best for me.

'Do you need to go?'
'Yes.'
'Then go!'

If only it were that simple. I felt torn.

It was around midnight. Almost an hour had passed since I took my sister's call, and I still hadn't left the house. Sitting in front of the mirror, wiping away a steady flow of tears as I tried to fix my blotchy, emotion-filled face and tired, cried-out eyes. I told myself to breathe. *Calm. Breathe.*

My reflection and I stared at each other, studying each other closely as I searched the parts that looked like the woman who now lay on her potential deathbed. I was oblivious to the irony of staring at my reflection to see if I resembled a narcissist. As my fingers ran along the contours of my features, I saw her hands. They were her hands. I felt restless.

What to do? What to do?

Go to the hospital, piss everyone off, and confirm what a troublemaker I was or listen to my guts and do what I needed. And maybe what she needed? There was a strange and chaotic pool of emotion to wade through to answer that one.

Two of my children had a relationship with her, so they were upset and worried about her condition while having to deal with nervousness about my feelings, whether I had regrets, whether there'd be a massive scene—and how Grandad was coping with it all. As with anything to do with Mom and me, they had a lot to deal with at once.

I could pretend I had made it easy for them. I hadn't interfered with their relationship with Mom or put them in a position where they were forced to choose. Still, they knew I hated the contact, which upset me, so of course there was conflict within them. I had to balance my belief that Mom didn't deserve my children and grandchildren with honouring their ability to show forgiveness towards her and their desire for 'family'.

They've inherited a complex of issues that are nigh on impossible to unravel, and I am sorry for that. How could they ever be expected to navigate such a toxic dynamic or even start understanding the complexity between Mom and me? They were trapped in the middle, seeking the shelter and comfort of a 'normal' family life, whatever that was, but they had little chance, and any expectation was probably unfounded.

Being stuck between two colliding mountains, they would always get caught by flying rocks; mine were thrown emotionally and wildly whereas Mom launched strategically and if she couldn't land a direct strike, she knew how to get at me through them.

A Small Prayer

I closed my eyes and talked to God.

That's the word I use, but you don't have to. God, angels, the universe, inner spirit, Allah; it matters not what you call it. It's all in your heart and belly, not your mind because that's fiercely protected by ego. Our minds are full of bullshit beliefs and fears, which our egos don't want to let go of, so our mind and ego ring-fence all that by encouraging us to seek comfortable solutions and external approval, using a convenient strategy—they protect themselves by pleasing everyone else.

This is a recurrent theme in my story, so make a note:

Talk to your heart and your belly and listen. They have all the answers and don't get it wrong. Ever.

Composure was restored. A remarkable sense of peace washed over me, and I knew what I had to do. I would go to the hospital but not until the right time, and my heart and belly would know when that was. Instead of getting dressed, I slipped into bed, closed my eyes, and immediately fell into a deep sleep, a sure indication that I had made the right decision.

3 a.m., Wednesday, 22 December 2021

I was woken up by the sound of my phone ringing again. My cousin had been researching Mom's condition, and she was calling to update me. I hadn't slept for long, but I'd had enough rest to take in what she wanted to share. She delivered her message with practical, solid sentences that I could understand, appreciate, and process.

There it was—clarity.

Shortly before sunrise, I got into my car and set off for the hospital. There was no sense of panic or restlessness, no nerves at all. I felt calm. Then, it occurred to me that I didn't know which hospital she was in. Calling my sister or Dad was not an option. This was a stealth mission. It was private and had nothing to do with anyone else. There weren't many hospitals to choose from, so I would start with the most likely and go from there.

As I approached the hospital, I scrutinised myself and felt sucked into the needy state of seeking approval. It doesn't take much for me to slip back into the mindset of the lonely child who'd been left to get on with things on their own: a state of confusion, of keeping things together but secretly yearning for love, comfort, and consistency while negotiating the harsh truth that I'm the only one who can provide myself with the shelter, love, and validation that every person wants.

It was God time again.

Listen to your heart, Dawn. Listen to your gut.

I thought about my mother.

Slow your breathing and listen to your heart. Set the intention. Feel the outcome.

Don't consider the how—that's not your job.

Let the outcome go, and dive, soul-deep, into faith. Just trust.

Set your vibration. Feel genuinely satisfied.

There was only one outcome, and that was to see her. I didn't know why, and I didn't know how, but I had faith that it was the right thing to do and that I'd achieve it.

You must keep it pure; pure intention from a place of pure love—no point-proving, no ego-feeding, and no agenda. You know when you're in pure love. You feel it. It's a sense of deep satisfaction in your heart.

Then, listen for the inspiration that follows.

Take another note: Only ever take inspired action from a place of purity.

I arrived at the hospital, then the thought hit me as I got out of my car. In December 2021, hospitals were still steeped in regulations and pandemic culture, which meant masks, sanitiser, social distancing, and suspicion of every surface. Bodies naturally responded, recoiling from contact with everything and everyone, and Mom was in a Covid ward. What the fuck was I doing?

It's early, and the staff will be busy. They'll never let me in. I don't really want to visit a Covid ward. I ignored the thoughts because thoughts aren't always honest. What I knew was that I was going to see her, and it would be okay.

The staff at reception confirmed that she was there. *I'm at the right hospital. Thank fuck for that.* They directed me to the ward.

I rang the ward buzzer. *Breathe.*

A voice asked me who I was. *Breathe.*

I then gave my mom's name. *Breathe.*

I waited.

The door opened, and I was ushered through. I was protected with gloves, gown, mask, and face shield—no chances taken—and guided to her ward door. The stars had aligned, vibrations had been raised, love had moved mountains, and the intention had been consummated. My mother was on the other side of that door. No need for fuss, nothing to fight, and nothing to be fearful of. What had changed? How had my emotional state evolved from confusion and turbulence into a place of calm, clarity, and decisiveness?

Self-doubt and indecisiveness stem from a feeling of not being valid or worthy enough to act. The first step is to be brave enough to lean into becoming comfortable with being an ordinary person because being an ordinary person is enough. There's no need to be a superhero, and you don't have to try to be one.

Ordinary people do extraordinary things, and that magic happens not from trying to be extraordinary. It happens from accepting and allowing themselves to live according to their purpose as ordinary people doing their best to do what they must do from a place of love.

When we act in harmony with our purpose, listening to our heart and belly, there's no need for fuss, friction, or fear because we are satisfied that we are where we are supposed to be and doing what we are supposed to be doing.

If you're feeling stuck at a crossroads, have faith in yourself, and trust in your instinctive ability to do what you are supposed to do. Imagine the last time you did something that made you feel happy and satisfied, because we experience a sense of calm at such times. Let's suppose we can reproduce that feeling; the way I do it is to place my hand over my heart, close my eyes, and pay attention to my breathing, and this allows me to move into that space where I can listen to what my heart and belly are saying.

You might use a different technique, but getting into this habit can help you find clarity when feeling confused.

I entered the door.

A more pitiful sight could not have been seen. Unkempt, pale, and uncomfortable. The excess of her body lay spilt and splayed across the hi-tech hospital bed, while the many machines and monitors that were attached to her beeped and burped furiously.

The inflammation and copious amounts of mucus in her lungs made it hard for her to breathe effectively. Her oxygen levels were dangerously low, so they were pumping it into her desperately to prevent suffocation. It irritated me that the ill-fitted CPAP mask she was wearing had become misplaced and was covering her eyes so she couldn't open them. *Am I the only one seeing this? Hello?* They couldn't hear my thoughts, and I had to resist the temptation to make a fuss.

'Mom, it's Dawn.'

'Dawn? My daughter Dawn?'

Her swollen hand scrummaged out from under the blanket and reached out. I held it gently; she held mine back. And there it was. That rare, shared space between us where the truce was unspoken but agreed upon, where nobody was around for her to perform. There were no points to score to justify behaviour or fuel the feud.

Despite everything, Mom was driven by the need for attention, and ultimately, I had delivered. I had got in my car at the crack of dawn and despite all odds, entered a Covid ward to see her.

Ordinarily, she would have seen this moment as either an opportunity to punish and reject me, had the right audience been front-row, or as an ultimate basking moment as the centre of attention. Somehow, they weren't on her agenda, not that morning. That morning was pure. That morning was honest, which is not something often associated with her. The woman who gave me life, provided the vessel of my being, beat me, loved me, used me, lied about me, empowered me, tried to break me, punished me, confused me, emotionally blackmailed me, liberated me, manipulated me, and so many other things that I could list, was now being honest with me?

The Truth Laid Bare

This once strong woman lay entrapped within the confines of a failing self-abused body, which exposed her spectacular greed and proudly presented the fruits of her life's commitment to using illness as a get-out-of-jail card and a constant source of attention.

Oh, Mom. What have you done to yourself?
Has all the inflicted misery, swallowed bitterness, spat-out resentment, outrageous lies, incessant greed, calculated manipulation, uncontrollable insecurity, and psychotic hunger for control come to consume you now?
Has the narcissistic arrogance that allowed you to believe you'd dodge all the bullets and forever be victorious been beaten into submission?

As I looked upon the ultimate manifestation of self-destruction, amounting to unintentional physical sabotage, while seeping from every pore, flowing through every artery and vein, and steering every blood cell, the fatal poison of resentment and revenge in all its glory was consuming the woman whom I'd emotionally and physically rejected and who had rejected me back... I felt nothing but compassion for her.

But not one ounce of guilt.
Not one hint of regret.
I knew.

I knew I had dodged bullets by retreating as often as I had. I could just as easily have gone to war and won with truth and justice on my side. I'd fought that war for decades. In more recent years, instead, I'd avoided as much poison as possible by walking away. The magnitude of her treatment of others and herself was on full display and plain to see in that hospital bed.

The ill-fitted CPAP mask was replaced. It was a relief to see her eyes, those eyes that could switch from laughter to spite on a flip of a coin. There wasn't any spite in them that morning. I probably couldn't go as far as saying there was kindness—I doubt she'd practised that enough—but her eyes were soft.

The most remarkable thing was the honesty and security in not having to say the usual forced, expected things that don't come close to expressing true feelings. Sometimes words are too small, only capable of pointing to the truth rather than nailing it. No words can fully deliver the sensation of a fistful of salt on an open wound. No words can capture the feeling of being embraced by a loved one or reunited with a lost child. And no words could fully express the communication I shared with my mother silently that morning. Sometimes the gut wins where words are useless.

Laying Down the Sword

This was pure knowing. Two women, who'd battled for decades, sitting together, each knowing all there was to know. This was a mutually agreed truce based on shared respect for being each other's worthy opponents, a tipping of the hat in acknowledgement that we'd battled well. This was our dram of whiskey to mark the coming of the end.

It was inexplicably comfortable and familiar, an intimacy that, by definition, could only be felt and understood by us. But the moment was tinged with something else. I knew I could put down my sword and shield because I had won, which simultaneously brought about feelings of relief and trauma. Perhaps 'tragic' is the word I'm looking for; to see a woman as formidable and majestic as my mother lying there, utterly defeated, was tragic.

I didn't have her treasures to look forward to, but I was healthy, happy, loved, satisfied, and whole. I have a different kind of treasure that money can't buy. It doesn't matter because my smile shines through my eyes from the happiness of my soul. That's where ordinary people are extraordinary. The real treasure isn't measured in cars, houses, and diamonds. Staying true to the soul and letting it shine brightly—that's where the real wealth is. That's why it's such a fallacy to measure success purely on money. Why do you think so many rich people are miserable? Nail self-satisfaction first. Then, when any money follows, you have the ultimate success—the best of both worlds without selling your soul.

I wonder, if she'd tamed me, whether things would have been different? Yes, probably, but not for her. Her plight would have remained the same, but my soul would have been sold. My cost would have been higher. She knew this, and so did I.

It doesn't sound much, holding a hand, but it was. Not her offering it. Rather, my accepting it. People either fight or flee. I had always fought. Anger and rage were my bodyguards against all the hurt until I reached a point where I wanted to change, grow, and evolve, so I worked on it as much as possible. I worked on forgiveness, and to be brutally honest, I hadn't wholly managed at that point. Still, I had discovered a version of forgiveness. I'd knocked down some walls and found compassion for her. Not so long ago, I even managed to call and say sorry for any pain I'd caused her. I was happy to have evolved enough to do that, with no expectation of anything in return because it was as much for my healing as anything else, but there was a consequence.

I could only manage forgiveness from afar. Removing anger exposed vulnerability. My frontal lobe didn't quite know what to do with that, so over the last few years, flight happened every time I'd been in her presence, and I could not let her physically touch me. I think I'd rather have died than accept her touch!

The frontal lobe's job is to plan behavioural responses to external and internal situations. Of course, others are far more qualified than me to explain this, but I can share my experience. In lay terms, my inability to accept physical contact from her was coming from my body with no input from my cerebral cortex whatsoever. There was no access to reasoning. No matter how irrational or how much I wanted to change things, I could not accept her physical contact. My body, driven by an urge to repulse, punish, and reject, wouldn't allow it, and my mind had no say in it.

But that morning, we broke bread. We held hands. It was simple—pure—and there was no urge to fight or flee. Peace enveloped me. Calm protected me.

The Covenant

Then, there was our pact. You see, my mother was incredibly clever, a world-class predator who knew precisely what she was doing. She could smell weakness and would strike for advantage with leopard-like stealth.

There were rules. Try to have her over, and you'd be a dead man walking, but play by her rules and rewards were dangled. I deliberately use that word, 'dangled', because she used her wealth as a carrot and stick to get her way. The truth is, I think we all thought she'd take advantage, take our souls, and then live forever!

Either way, it wasn't worth it for me. I'm not even sure that assessment came from an honourable place. I think I'd always assumed I'd be an old lady when her time was up, and by then, I wouldn't have any use or care for all those diamonds. I have been more than happy to make my own fortune and buy my own treasures. On the other hand, my dad and sister are a narcissist's dream, so rewards for good behaviour were firmly on the table.

It was a straight trade. She knew they appeased her. She knew there was an agenda, and she knew there was lip service; however, that was the deal, and she agreed to it because they also served her needs. Except it also fed her insecurities because there was never complete trust. How could there be? Even though it was embroiled with love, albeit a fucked-up kind of love, it was still a transaction, and insecure people smell that a mile off.

I may have been her nemesis because I couldn't be controlled and wouldn't serve her needs, but I could be trusted, and trust was what she needed that morning. She knew she could count on me to act with her best interests at heart because she also knew I had nothing to gain from her not being around.

A few years ago, she made me promise that I would always see her right in medical situations. Since then, she rejected my offer to be there with her, but still, for me, a promise is a promise, so I had a duty to honour it when given a chance.

That promise wasn't the reason I came to the hospital that morning, although it provided me with a convenient guise to hide behind. If not for that reason, then why? Because she's my mother and I loved her? No, not really. I'm not sure 'love' is the right word to use here because my interpretation of love bore no relationship to my experience with her.

It was just something I had to do, almost as instinctive as scratching an itch or brushing my hair out of the way of my eyes. It was purely instinctive, a sense of duty, perhaps, regardless of any promise.

The Conqueress Concedes

Mom broke the silence.

'The doctors said I was doing well?'

'Do you want the truth?' I asked.

'You've never hidden from telling me the truth before. I see no reason to start now.'

As soon as I heard those words, they became chiselled on my heart, where they will remain forever. Mom had never admitted I was a truth teller—certainly not while we weren't friends!

Sounds like nothing, right?

Imagine being accused of lying throughout your whole life and enduring a childhood where you often didn't dare tell the truth. When I had lied, it was to try to avoid punishment or stemmed from panic about her unpredictable wrath. Sometimes it was to piss her off if obstinance had kicked in, and in that childish naivety, I'd also effectively handed over the complete set of terms and conditions to her, so she could manipulate situations with her version of the truth, safe in the knowledge that Dad would always believe her and safe that I would be branded as dishonest.

Survival meant fine-tuning my instincts to question everything, ensuring there were always witnesses, and constantly seeking validation for anything I wanted to put forward as truth, which was mostly fruitless by the way—even external validation was made redundant for me.

Therefore, her admission of my truthfulness was accepted as a big fucking declaration!

In my mind, I gave thanks. It wasn't an apology, but it was an admission, and that's the crux of this book's message—to acknowledge the importance of validation, and then to consider how to survive when you don't get it and to learn a way to negotiate around wanting validation rather than needing it.

Having reached a point where I didn't need it, the person who stole it all from me had finally given it back—the ultimate irony. It was a point score to me, and I was grateful, but the sad thing is that it was also the least victorious win I'd ever had.

A Fight for Life

I gave her the truth.

'Your oxygen is too low. They are forcing the maximum amount possible through the CPAP mask, and they can't put you on a ventilator as that will kill you. If we don't get the oxygen level up, they will withdraw treatment, and you have a DNR [Do Not Resuscitate] in place.'

After a slight pause, I put the ball in her court. 'What do you want to do? Are you ready to go, or do we sort this out?'

She looked slightly alarmed.

'No, I'm not ready to go.'

'Okay. We have some work to do then. Do you remember, you helped me breathe when I was in labour? That's what we need to do for you now.'

As I spoke to her, I could sense a change in her facial expression. Something wasn't sitting right with her.

'I haven't agreed to a DNR. Who agreed to that?'

There was a hint of the familiar fire in her eyes—*how dare they decide for me?* I had to give it to her straight, and she had to listen carefully and follow instructions.

'The doctors decided. Medically, they have no choice, so you must focus because that machine needs to consistently read ninety-two at the very least, and you're way below. If we don't sort that out, they will withdraw treatment, and that's the end.'

She was listening.

'How long have I got to make that happen?'

The truth.

'Ideally, this morning. Maximum twenty-four hours.'

CHAPTER TWO
Tick Tock Tick Tock

The Choice

Imagine you had twenty-four hours to make a final decision to live or die. No time for chasing wistful dreams and wishes or considering your comfort zone; instead, deciding whether to fight. Deciding whether to live.

In Mom's case, the decision to fight would mean talking to her blood cells, orchestrating her chemistry, and deciding to reduce viral infection. It would mean high oxygen intake to ensure her body wouldn't produce carbon monoxide and poison itself. That decision would mean blocking the option of withdrawing medical care.

Put yourself in that position. You have twenty-four hours. You choose. Do you have the belly for that? Do you have the stamina, the determination, and the grit? Have you already lived your life and found yourself in a place where you're satisfied, fulfilled, and happy to go?

Maybe, you're worn out, war-torn, and resentful, and in such case, ready to give up? Or are your heels screeching to stop death, and your whole essence turns into a resounding 'NO! Not ready. Dying isn't an option,' with preparedness to do whatever it takes? If so, why?

Are you not ready because of your regrets? Because you haven't 'finished'?

Are you terrified?

If we've lived a well-filled life, have faith, and come to terms with and found peace with what death means—whether we believe there is an afterlife or not—then, in theory, indeed, we'd be happy to accept the end of our physical time.

The Power of Hard Truths

It's a hard-hitting thought, not one that's easy to be comfortable with, and that's part of the problem. Nobody pushes the hard truths. Mostly, we are encouraged to avoid them, which is much easier, except it's not really because when we only seek the lovely stuff, we struggle to sustain it. The benefits are short-lived.

How often have you read a great quote, bought a good course, or tried self-development without applying a single bit of it? It's not because you're too ordinary or not worthy. It's just because you haven't taken some steps beforehand. I trust that the hard-hitting stuff will reinforce just how extraordinary you are and therefore reinforce permission to follow your dreams.

I promise you, with all my heart, that if you can make peace with the hard stuff, dealing with the rest will be much easier, setting you free to be your best self in a completely sustainable way. I promise, so please stay with me. Relief is coming.

Now that I have your attention on death, one of our most brutal truths, how does that help? It changes the weight you give to the validation you receive from others, right? How important might other people's opinions be to you in your final hours?

Let's take all the negative self-talk and criticism that protects you from doing what you want and apply them amidst your final regrets at the end of your time. Let's give those thoughts a grilling and check how worthy they are.

You didn't have a great childhood. You weren't popular at school. You're scared of public speaking, you've had your heart broken a few times, your kid rejected you, you've got some regrets... So what? Irrelevant. Those things are unimportant in your final twenty-four hours, but why wait until you're on your deathbed? The secret is to let those things go while you can still make different decisions, so regret can't touch you and you gain peace and fulfilment for the rest of your life AND in your final hours. Just in this alone, your spirit starts to rise. How marvellous is that?

I know we all think we appreciate time, but we don't. We articulate the notion of time at the surface level; we acknowledge the concept of it. We like inspiring quotes on social media about quality time and read books about time efficiency, time management, and life balance. We regurgitate how important it is, and then what? Not a lot. We continue to waste the time we have.

Because there's no urgency.

The Shit We Indulge In

We indulge in our fears, beliefs, and ego with excuses about all the things that stand in our way when it's all bullshit.

'Indulge' is such a provocative word, isn't it? It's fine when we apply it to a pleasant experience and accept it when we treat ourselves. Still, it doesn't feel very comfortable when attached to anything relating to our behaviour or the truth about our wants and needs. We automatically start to defend ourselves against looking like we're spoilt or entitled.

We might indulge unconsciously and habitually, but when it comes to our beliefs and ego, the bottom line is that we all do it. Yes, ladies and gentlemen, headline news—we are all indulgent brats for beliefs and ego!

You can pretty it up. You can unpack years of experiences and everything that has influenced you that justify your beliefs—parents, teachers, friends, money, popularity, culture, religion, abuse, and trauma to name a few of the usual suspects. That will explain the whys and wherefores, justify how you interact with the world, qualify the terms and conditions set within your relationships, and how you communicate with yourself internally.

Let's look at some of these. Lay them out on the table.

Look at how we shit-talk ourselves:

- 'I'm scared.'
- 'I'm nobody.'
- 'I'm worthless.'
- 'Nobody is interested in what I have to say.'
- 'I'm not qualified or educated.'
- 'I'm too old.'
- 'I'm too young, too fat, too skinny, too rich, too poor, too proud, black, female, gay, ugly, dyslexic...'

How poorly treated we were:

- 'My parents never loved me.'
- 'My teachers said I wouldn't amount to anything.'
- 'I didn't have any friends.'
- 'My partner treated me like shit.'
- 'I was bullied.'

The stuff that's happening now:

- 'My boss takes advantage.'
- 'Nobody considers my feelings.'
- 'My family treats me like a doormat.'
- 'This world is so unfair. Where's my break?'

Then, there are the 'what ifs':

- 'What if people laugh.'
- 'What if people don't like me.'
- 'What if I get criticised.'
- 'What if someone posts something negative about me on social media.'

Other creative ways to tell ourselves that success is a terrible idea:

- 'If I did well, my family might think I've betrayed them, my friends might not like that I've elevated myself, and my partner might prefer me not to have any attention.'

We need to face these thoughts and feelings, and then face how ridiculous they are.

Then, the terrifying ones:

- 'What if they think I'm something special?'
- 'What if I think I'm something special?'

But the outcome remains the same. None of it is important, permanent, or relevant to how you go forward. It's bullshit. The reason it's still with you, dogging you, holding you back, and causing you unhappiness is that you don't have the right amount of urgency or a compelling enough reason to let some of this stuff go.

Use Your Vision to Your Advantage

Please don't avoid the image of your final hours. Sit, close your eyes, and create the experience in your mind as vividly as possible. Feel the sense of urgency and sit in that uncomfortable space. Breathe in the tension, feel the urgency and weight of it, lean into any panic, and reject any temptation not to connect with this thought. Breathe.

If you picked up this book, something in your heart and belly is telling you something:

'Hey, ordinary person, you are special. You are also extraordinary and glorious. But your spirit is being held down like a cork in water—

you need to let the cork go. You need to let it rise!'

Your extraordinariness is not measured by external validation, and nothing on your list of bullshit beliefs or protective pillars will be there to save your life, but they will hold you back from living it.

Put your hand on your heart and ask, *What do I want? Love of myself, inner peace, no regrets?*

Instead of listening to your beliefs and inner chitter chatter, talk to your heart and your belly and listen to what they have to say. They have all the answers and never get it wrong. Ever. If you didn't write that down when I first said it, now's your chance.

Teamwork—a Force to be Reckoned With

I sat at Mom's bedside for nearly four hours, and we set to work on breathing. It took a little time to find the right tempo that would allow her to increase her oxygen intake without causing a massive coughing episode.

We also fell into our rhythm of being in each other's space. It was comfortable and soothing despite the gravity of the challenge. We had one common goal and just got right on it. We listened to Neil Diamond songs, chatted, took the piss out of each other a little, and swapped some simple truths.

I can see why this is very confusing, given our history. You aren't supposed to get it. It's an exclusive understanding, a private club. When we fought each other, it was a serious clash of titans; however, we were an unbreakable alliance when we fought on the same side. On that day, fighting to bring Mom's oxygen levels up, we were on the same side.

I can also see why this pisses my sister off. I know she has invested so much of herself in seeking Mom's approval and attention. She'd see it as me swanning in as I please, breaking the rules, and doing what I like. When you add in that, given the right circumstances, the warmth between my mother and me can't be tampered with or replicated by any of those who have appeased her, I can see how bloody annoying that must be.

To hand over all your validation to others—even your mother—is trading self-worth, inner approval, and the decisions you make for yourself. You might think this is an easy trade; however, you give away your soul, and that cost far outweighs the return on investment. It's a bad deal.

The Lies We Fall For

Have you honestly considered how many decisions you make for the approval of others? As children, we seek approval from pretty much everyone we encounter—parents, siblings, family, peers, friends, and teachers. It's a habit we form as babies, and it works. Get the approval of others, and we're popular and loved—*yeah!*

That's marvellous for society and for curbing children's behaviour. Really! It's a great strategy and brings lots of happiness as we lap up that acceptance, approval, and affection. We forget that it often also squashes dreams, slowly extinguishing our inner fires as we absorb the insecurities and unhappiness of those influential people we encounter.

An unhappy mother strips her children of confidence as it exposes her insecurities. Or the abusive father who never had the tools to express positive emotion, so he dominated using physicality. Don't forget the irritated teacher who never made it in what they wanted, bitterly resented having to teach, and took it out on their students.

As children, we naively embrace the insecurities of those adults, thinking grownups know everything—another one of the biggest cons in life.

Maybe, it's time for a fresh look at how many adults really have their shit together, and within that reckoning, consider how much of their behaviour, driven by their bullshit beliefs, we have inherited. How much of that do we pass down to our children? This shit's generational. If no one breaks that cycle, it just goes on and on, and nothing changes.

As we discover the truth and realise how little value the validation sought from others holds, can we consider finding our own approval and validation, permitting ourselves to be who we want to be?

A Glimpse of Mom

The consultant came to talk to Mom. What followed was one of the most elegant conversations I have ever witnessed, and I was satisfied that she knew exactly what her position was, what the choices were, why, and what had to happen to prevent withdrawal of care. It was also made clear that if she wanted the CPAP mask removed, they would agree, which would be the end.

She smacked the consultant on his hand, with that well-rehearsed glint in her eye, her flirtatious smoulder still able to splutter through her swollen face.

'Well, bloody well mend me then!'

There she was.

My extraordinary mother. Her body was failing, but her spirit was sturdy. You've got to laugh—and respect where it's due for the audacity! She genuinely didn't give a shit who she was talking to or how serious the situation was. Her charm offensive kicked in, regardless. She knew what she wanted and assumed someone would make that happen. Ultimate entitlement. She unapologetically abuses her physicality to suit her need for attention and assumes someone else will mend it.

A Peaceful Parting

On the upside, it was explained that she had a fifty-fifty chance of walking out of the hospital and that older, more critically ill people had succeeded. Moving forward, they would take it twenty-four hours at a time.

It took a few hours, but she was comfortable when I left. Her eyes weren't swollen, she knew what she had to do, and her oxygen saturation level fluctuated between eighty-nine and ninety-one per cent consistently. There was peace between us, and I left her better than I'd found her.

Peace—an interesting energy, considering the context. We didn't exchange 'love' sentences. We didn't shed any tears. We didn't say any final goodbyes.

What? I hear you think. Nobody said, '*I love you*'?

No. We didn't need to. Our familiar rhythm and mutual respect were enough. And that was simply perfect.

You see, distorting truth to her advantage was one of her strongest skills. She was a grandmaster manipulator—a world-class spin doctor. She could extract your deepest secrets and store them for years, then weaponised them, recreating a version that would sound so convincing that it'd make you question it yourself.

That's why the pureness of our time together didn't require such an inconsequential exchange of the word 'love'. She was a narcissist in all its glory. Her measure of love was based on how much adoration you showed her. I hadn't done that. I had rejected her, and she wouldn't have accepted that sentence without introducing some sort of tone.

My measure of love sits within a less manipulative space, with an exchange of generosity, truth, respect and caring for one another, which isn't exactly her flavour. I doubt I'd have accepted it if she'd said it.

The perfection was there because we didn't need to fill the space with expected emotional exchanges. Neither of us had ever lived our lives doing expected things. Neither of us would seek approval or validation. Nobody expects you to understand. Both of us would probably giggle at the fact that we didn't care either way.

The sense of comfort and peace between us just was. Existing within its own beauty of honesty. It was beautiful because those words didn't happen, and I wouldn't change a single thing.

7 a.m., Sunday, 26 December 2021

I was woken by my sister's name flashing up on the phone. For the split second before I answered, I knew—why else would I get a call from her at that early time?

'She's gone'.

Confusion swarmed through my whole body.

She was doing well. Oxygen levels were consistently up. She was even eating the 'vile porridge they keep presuming is edible'.

How? Why? Everything about this outcome contradicted everything about her, conflicted with how I left her and contradicted how the nurses reported her improvement over those last few days. She had bought herself another four days since I had visited. How can she be gone?

Undefeated

What the actual fuck?! She had asked for the CPAP mask to be removed and wanted to go, but let's have it right—nothing killed her. Nothing 'took' her. She'd kept her fight record; she didn't lose any battle.

She chose. As with everything she'd ever done, on her terms, her rules, not seeking anyone else's permission, and not looking for any external validation. To the end, she knew who would serve her—she didn't call me to assist with those fatal decisions. She was cleverer than that, and always knew who would get her what she wanted.

An Alternative Perspective on Time

I will never view twenty-four hours the same again.

We give way to dreamy plans, then snatch them back immediately with our bullshit sentences:

- 'I'd love to…'
- 'I wish I could…'
- 'One day, I'll…'
- 'When I have more time, I'll…'
- 'When I can afford it, I'll…'
- 'When the economy picks up, I'll…'

In the meantime, we become entrenched in life—marriage, children, work, building businesses, running a home—and before we know it, we haven't honoured ourselves. We've forgone our heart's desire and sunk our spirit.

We become influenced by other ways to measure extraordinariness and gloriousness—money, property, cars, saving a world problem—and society's focus on external validation reinforces the belief that just because we live everyday lives, we are somehow not capable. Still, the truth is that this has no bearing on your gloriousness. Not. One. Bit.

We forget the dreams we had, the promises we made, and the things we were determined to reach for, and we settle into the humdrum of life while the clock ticks. We forget it all until our final days when regret resurrects our hearts' desires. By then, it's too late.

I've been quite hard-hitting, so let me soothe you with some balance.

Firstly, there's no sadness with my mother's end. There's not much she'd have done differently; she embraced all her good and bad and lived true to herself, no matter what, so it was a well-lived life and a chosen end. She even managed to get annoyed with the doctors in those final hours. She decided she wanted to go, but it didn't happen quickly enough for her liking, and even on her death bed, told them to sort it out and hurry it up.

Secondly, there is no wasted time, and I acknowledge how contradictory that sounds, so I will explain. You see, if you're not in the right mindset to take those steps forward, attempts will be forced and futile. Many gurus will use clever sentences and ways to leverage 'IMMEDIATE ACTION' but often, they have a course to sell you. How to sort the mindset out in the first place is often left out.

Those years of non-action aren't wasted. They are an investment in lessons, the development of wisdom, and an education in what makes you happy or unhappy. Neither should you ever discredit or regret the unhappy bits and mistakes because, without those, you'll never know how not to do things.

Tap Into Your Glory

Contrast is marvellous. Adversity is education for the soul and delivers all the answers, but it doesn't happen overnight. We must first recognise that it gets hard before it gets easy. Often, the more adversity you've experienced, the harder the ego works to protect you. Its sole job is to keep you in your comfort zone, hence the negative self-talk. If you can stop comparing yourself to others, stop looking for external validation, and stop defending or excusing yourself, you can start tapping into your glory.

Close your eyes and breathe. Find satisfaction in your heart, smile until you feel it in your organs, and listen to inspired thoughts—and do this regardless of your circumstances. Please note that the whole point of validating yourself is NOT to be distracted by any external 'stuff'.

The urgency, as forementioned, isn't to make you do anything but to recognise yourself—how amazing all humans are, what a miracle you are—and to seek your heart's desire and start making decisions based on that.

You haven't wasted time. You've simply gathered all that you need. Once you start validating yourself, regardless of your life thus far, you'll feel everything. Your heart and belly will tell you every detail and never get it wrong, and if you feel as though you've heard me say this before, good. I'm going to keep reminding you of this.

I know you won't want to let go and trust your gut, and you'll feel much resistance. Still, to release the shackles and validate yourself, you must let go of relying on anything external to provide that safety. Instead, you must find satisfaction DESPITE your circumstances. The glory of being ordinary lends to this because you have nothing to lose. The world press is not watching you, ready to report anything.

Get a piece of paper and write down all those sentences going through your mind:

- 'Yes, but this happened to me…'
- 'What nobody understands is this…'
- 'But what about this?'
- 'Surely, I deserve to feel worried/worthless/frustrated?'

Yes, sweetheart. I get it. Life does produce comfort zones, fear of change, and lack of confidence. It makes you feel like an imposter, and I understand why you want to run and hide in the warm blanket of avoidance.

But 'deserve'? No, you don't deserve a starved soul. You deserve glory.

Or do nothing. Stay shielded under an umbrella. It'll keep you dry whether it's raining or not, and that's fine too, but can I give it to you straight? Let me tell you the truth, as I did to my mother: death is not the only way that living ends. You're not genuinely living if you're not true to yourself, and when your time comes, that umbrella won't save you.

We don't talk enough about death. It isn't often celebrated. We decide it's only okay if someone hasn't been snatched away too young or too tragically. Unfortunately, we can only hypothesise about what happens next because of the very nature of the end of life and the fact that we are all alive. We can confirm that our body and our organs die. What we will never know until after the fact is whether there's anything else. Literally, not one person knows, not for sure!

What I do know is that if we can try to view life differently, stop putting the measure of time upon it, and change our perspective first, then maybe we can view death differently—both our final day and those of our loved ones.

The grief of losing a loved one is simply the love we have left over. Resentment is also a form of grief—the grief of losing ourselves while we still have the chance to change our outcomes and live fully.

Instead of avoiding some truth and choosing to remain in unfulfillment,

- Could you choose to avoid regret?
- Could you choose to accept and love the lessons?
- Could you choose to live?

I trust I can hear you say, 'I want to live.'

Well, go on then—you only need your permission.

To include me in this and not be a hypocrite, what were my 'sentences'? Here's one for starters:

One day, I'll write a book.

Although I'd probably tried a hundred times, I never got past the first thousand or so words. I always thought, *when it's right, it'll come.* Well, the time is right, and the time has come, so here I am—vulnerable, exposed, putting my heart's art out there to be judged by others but doing it anyway.

An ordinary person, an indomitable spirit, unstoppable, unapologetically doing what she wants to raise her soul and fill her heart.

A mom, wife, a middle-aged woman who's done very well for herself but a far cry from being a billionaire or a world leader!

If I were to cave into society's notion of what a credible author looks like, someone like me might ask themselves, *Who the hell wants to hear what such an ordinary person like me has to say?!*

An indomitable spirit says, 'Fuck that! I have every right to author a book.'

Despite not living in a mansion or having a Grammy or a Nobel award—despite being ordinary—I know I'm also bloody glorious.

I am kind, have integrity, am great at business, and love people. I love talking to them, listening to them, and exploring how they think—discovering what makes them happy or sad, what their dreams are, what they are great at, and what they are awful at.

Based on the many other ordinary people I talk to, I've concluded that we make a lot more sense than many who are much more prominent and renowned than us, so why shouldn't the voice of an ordinary person be heard?

I'm writing this book first and foremost because doing it is making ME happy and fulfilling something within me. That means more than whether anyone will like it.

And I know it's scary shit that I am asking you to consider; however, I'd love it if you would join me on this journey with your version of what makes you happy:

Ordinary people validating themselves, approving of themselves.

Ordinary people joining in each other's glory.

Ordinary people becoming extraordinary with indomitable spirits.

CHAPTER THREE

Our Compass
to Our Compass

I finished the last chapter with an invitation to join me, as an ordinary person, on the brave journey of self-discovery in a way that makes personal development sustainable—in a way that helps you to literally apply self-help.

Will you come along?

'Yes, please', some of you will be saying. 'We will join in. Let's hold hands, celebrate our human inadequacies, and maybe even sing 'Kumbaya' around a fire with flowers in our hair.'

I can also imagine the rest of you rolling your eyes just a little bit, thinking, *Well, Mrs Clever Clogs, will you tell us what to do next, now that you've made us feel like shit? I suppose you'll be so very predictable and tell us about forgiveness. Well, you need not bother—like we don't already know that. Don't you think we've tried that?*

Well, no flowers, fire dancing or forgiveness. Not yet.

Don't be disappointed. The celebration of human connection is bloody lovely, and the euphoria within those ceremonial collaborations feels rapturous; but, unfortunately, it's also like a drug. Following the high of celebration, you come down, feeling like you've failed as you slide back into old habitual inner talk. You have also started an addiction.

Why do you think so many people buy course after course, attend seminar after seminar, and do nothing with all that learning? It's because they've jumped in too quickly, and it's the addiction to those human gatherings and the feel-good factor that they're feeding, not because of the content being sold. That said, it's imperative to seek improvement, and those resources are incredibly valuable but not if you're going to waste them. All you're doing is making yourself feel incapable in your inability to keep it up, and in your fall, giving those who you bought from a bad reputation.

Sort the perspective out first. You can have the greatest business idea or meet the best love partner in the world, but if your perspective is off, it'll never work.

I'm not here to sell you a dream. I'm here to sell you yourself—and then you can help yourself to your dreams. When you then invest in yourself, you'll apply it and be able to sustain it, so you need to put your flowers aside for a moment.

We all need a compass and some navigation, but, unfortunately, it becomes hard to know where to turn. Resources are abundant online, and I don't know about you, but it's all starting to sound like lots of noise to me.

I ponder why things are so much worse now. Seemingly everyone suffers from one thing or another—imposter syndrome, unworthiness, childhood trauma, fear of change—all struggling to hold on by the tips of our fingers and scrabbling for certainty.

When I look back at the history of humanity, I wonder how the cavemen coped. What did they do? Have you ever thought about that? Life was brutal. What did they have as a resource? It wasn't an influencer throwing motivational tips on the cave wall: 'Eight Ways to Take Back Your Power Against the Sabre Tooth Tiger' or 'Use Your Chakras to Sharpen Your Spear'.

Instead, they had the best resource ever. They had themselves. Pure grit and determination for survival. They bore ultimate indomitable spirits without being burdened with the ability to articulate self-deprecating thoughts such as I'm not worthy. Communication was no more than grunts, at least until we evolved into homo sapiens. I guess that would have simplified the inner talk!

I love the era in which I belong, but as I age, I crave a simpler, quieter inner sanctuary. I'm amusing myself a little, I bet I could create a grunting caveman retreat, a glamping cave experience, where we literally grunt to each other!

On a more serious note, have you noticed that the more we seek external validation, the worse it's getting? The sad thing is knowing that all the compass we need is within us—within our stories and our hearts.

All we need, we already have. We've just lost our ability to hear it, to feel it. We need to find a way to find a way.

Forgiveness will feature; however, there are a few things to consider before navigating to that, and I will get to those shortly.

Enough is Enough

Before anything, we must first decide enough is enough. Decide that what we have been doing thus far hasn't worked well enough and decide that we want to be brave enough to look in a different direction. Because as uncomfortable as we are with how things are, we may as well be uncomfortable but more satisfied. You may have reached this point many times before, but in the name of protection, the ego often steps in and talks you out of any sustainable action, and you don't really know why.

If you're not ready to decide that enough is enough, you have two choices: keep reading and come with me to explore, or don't. Put the book down, and be satisfied with your dissatisfaction until you're not, and I will patiently wait on your bookshelf. I will be here for when you reach a point where you know in your belly, where within every strand of your DNA you know you're settling, where you're going down the road leading to regret, resentment, and dissatisfaction. Where your insides are probably screaming quite loudly.

You can choose your heart attack, your frustrations and tiredness battling with a struggling business, a sparkless relationship, and a war-torn soul, OR choose your satisfaction, well-being, certainty, and strategy for your version of success. Choose to be able to take fear, understand it differently and turn it into action.

I'd love to take you down another road, one where each step you take can be trodden differently. Perhaps wearing slightly more elegant shoes, with a more rose-tinted view ahead, now that you've contemplated how much resentment and regret you may be stacking up, ready for your final days.

Pop an Opposite

Reaching the point of enough isn't the challenge. Once we get there, taking some action is where we fall. This is the first exploration of the other side of the story, having recognised that we need to take a different path. Commonly, this is the hurdle where things get muddled up. We feel that there's more, but that gets translated into 'I'm not being good enough' for whatever that 'more' is. This is the perfect time to 'pop an opposite'.

The truth is, if your heart didn't know you were more, you wouldn't feel dissatisfied. Having this frustration means that you ARE enough for more. Your heart and soul yearn more because YOU ARE MORE. So please stop your own bullshit, recognise the ego is just trying to keep you safe but is doing the opposite.

I want you to swallow 'enough is enough' hard. Taste that this IS you being enough, worthy enough, capable enough and brave enough. These sentences aren't new to you, but they are meaningless unless you know HOW to digest them.

How do we start to smoke out the stance of enough is enough in a way that delivers action? It's all in our story, where there are always two sides. I've described just a thimbleful of detail about my relationship with my mom, and it would be easy to write a whole epilogue about what it is to be the product of a narcissist. I could fill pages of horror stories—incredible childhood memories that those not exposed to such parenting would be aghast at. Kindred spirits would bask in recognition, acknowledging the torture that becomes the version of what love means when it's bestowed upon the children of such characters.

I could set up a Facebook community, and we could gather as children who've had parts of our souls stolen, eaten up by the energy required to survive such parents, and we could wallow in sorrow at what sad tales of woe we carry. We could dissect how it affected every other relationship we've had, including with ourselves, and how it's forever dented our existence and broken our hearts; spinning regurgitated versions of hurt, rejection, betrayal, subservience, lies, and manipulation from the very person we should have been able to seek shelter under.

Then, we could connect with other communities who have suffered, such as the children of addicts and abusers, and others who have experienced emotional inadequacies because they were raised by people who only knew how to perpetuate hurt.

We could extend this to include those who undertake grown-up toxic relationships, who've undone everything they had and can't stitch themselves back together again.

Fuck all that!

Please take note: I trust you are starting to pick up that the key is to do the opposite of what is expected or seems easy for a quiet life or to appease what other people think are the rules. Those rules are encouraged to make other people feel comfortable. God forbid we step outside our lanes and make anyone else feel inadequate.

Nor will the easy, quiet, or expected route work for you; it takes you to precisely the opposite of where you want to be. We use our stories to justify avoidance when the truth is, that this 'easy' route leads to worse results than if were brave enough to abandon the beliefs. If we feel fear or tempted to do what WE presume is what other people dignify as valid, we must recognise that and STOP, just for a moment, and look to do the opposite.

My Money, My Mouth, My Opposites

Here's a prime example of the point I am making. As I am sitting here with my laptop and writing these very words, my thoughts are veering off: *Fuck, I'm writing a whole book with no structure, purely instinctively and entirely off the cuff!*

Martin, my editor, started helping with structure, aiding and abetting, and I am happy to employ his skills and experience. Frankly, however, he stands very little chance of enforcing all his expertise, although, luckily, he has captured my approach well enough to adapt. Another opposite. We potentially held some differences of opinion, and it was this that attracted me to him.

I didn't seek to be appeased. That's not where the magic is. I didn't want a congruent opinion. I wanted the resistance. I wanted to challenge my ego, to have someone look for the faults. That's the point of the book, right? To be comfortable with that unapologetic imperfection.

It is possibly appropriate that fate knew what we agreed on, as, during this journey, he lost his beautiful boy, Matty. Almost serendipitously, we shared the intimacy of starting my book, which touches on death, while we were both dealing with loss.

I giggle a little and recognise my mother's audacity seeping through my veins. I'm writing this one sentence at a time. I don't know what the next chapter will be, and I can't edit the previous one until I've written the next one! What the fuck am I doing?

My thoughts wander…

I'm making myself incredibly happy, playing at being the author I'd love to be. Am I writing this book for me? Or for validation of others? If I'm writing it for me, then why should I follow the scripts Google offers—articles written by experts, who are selling a course that I abandoned any interest in within minutes?

I'll listen to Martin, but I already know I'll only take the bits I like and discard what doesn't make me feel happy and satisfied, even if that falls outside the 'rules'. Otherwise, it's not truly authentic, holds no boundary-breaking, and completely contradicts the purpose. I'm delighted to be an ordinary person, being gloriously curious about where my heart takes me. I have nothing to lose, apart from knowing I'll lose a part of my soul if I don't write or approach it in any other way other than following my heart, letting my indomitable spirit prance around these pages, choreographing sentences unapologetically.

Let me remind you: talk to your heart and your belly and listen to what they say. They have all the answers and never get it wrong. Ever.

Indulging the bullshit beliefs born from our childhood is not the message of this book, not this narrative—not my story.

Suppose we can detach ourselves for a moment. In that case, we find details of individual stories inconsequential because the results are everyone's story—regardless.

The Sweet Girl Next Door

Do you remember anyone you went to school with, such as the sweet girl you thought was picture-perfect? She has no more confidence than anyone else—she smiles sweetly to mask enormous inadequacy and willingly offers herself like a sacrificial virgin to avoid anyone noticing her outside of niceness.

She had a nice upbringing. No obvious trauma. Everything was censored and considered conservatively, cautiously. Her parents had a nice house, a neat garden, a sensible car, and safe jobs.

They loved her.

But she quickly learned who she had to be to feel approval and love; that solid, stable, sincere love; that vanilla, inexpressive, unimpressive, not very obvious love.

Those appeased parents, neighbours, and teachers thought and said, 'What a nice family. What a nice quiet child.'

That oppressed, compressed, depressed love, packaged and wrapped up in a neat, scared, constrained bow.

Did you envy her? Because all you'd seen was the external popularity, with no evidence of the internal oppression, conformity and need for external validation that would drive her decisions for the rest of her life.

She's just as fucked as anyone. She's just as dependent on other people's approval, and her fear is just as magnified as yours. No sensational story but the same results. Details don't matter. We live, die, and then the next generation cracks on. Rinse and Repeat.

Flip The Pancake

I want to park the predictable details. Instead, I want you to flip the story. If you can't find one, fine, you win the presidential suite of unfulfilled ordinariness. Your glory will sit with a crown of resentment and regret, and you get the magnificent death we call unfulfillment. That sounds damning, I know, but the truth is that it's far easier to flip a story than the beliefs that the story generates. If you can reverse your bullshit beliefs without identifying the story they were embedded in, good luck to you.

I don't want to dismiss you to make you feel awful. That's the complete opposite of how you sit in my heart. I don't want to listen because that can't help you. I want your spirit to rise. Indulging you doesn't do that.

In the meantime, I am here to talk to ordinary people who want to discover themselves through satisfying, wholesome decisions, and who like the nice things in life but aren't prepared to trade integrity or love for financial wealth and the falsehoods of fame.

I want to listen to ordinary people who may or may not have faced adversity but, either way, have found themselves unfulfilled and want to turn that around a little.

I seek the souls who yearn to be unapologetic for whatever they want, be it big or small, rich or modest.

I don't want to showcase the consequences of cruelty. Instead, I want to showcase the extraordinariness of ordinary people.

I want ordinary people to know they can have it all—love, money, security, happiness, confidence, and wholeness—without trading their souls. I want to spread a scripture of how holding onto fear and bullshit beliefs delivers the very opposite of, and worse than, what you're too afraid to do.

If you have faced horror, well, good for you because you've already walked through fire. With the right ethos, a dash of perspective, and a sprinkle of urgency, this will be an absolute breeze compared to trauma. You can already dance with the devil and survive, so you have nothing to fear.

I'm looking for ordinary people, front-line soldiers. We're the troops, the masses, the ordinary people who work hard to raise their children and exist within their communities by doing their best and doing the right thing but who, somewhere along the line, began to believe that they were too ordinary to be extraordinary; and so, I'm here to say,

'Hey!

Don't you realise?

Don't you realise how remarkable it is that you made it this far, that you're honest and good and have value?

That makes you glorious!

All you need to do is have a little faith and belief in yourself and know that you don't need anyone else to approve.'

This book is not for those who want to be indulged and felt sorry for, or those who want to stay comfortable.

Nor is it for those seeking all the noise about getting rich quickly and who believe that money or fame is a solid enough plaster to hold the seams together. Good luck with that, and I love anyone who reaches their interpretation of success, even millionaires and billionaires, but this book isn't about that. Although, ironically, do some of this work on your beliefs and perspective first, and you're more likely to be happy when you do make your millions—just saying!

This is for ordinary people who have had enough and want to stand up and be who they want to be, whether that means remaining in the gloriousness of ordinariness or even striving for money, wealth, or fame.

My story is that ordinary people get to have a lovely home and car, go on holiday, and wear nice clothes, and they get to carve out choices for themselves and their children.

They get to be loved and fulfilled and satisfied and fill their fucking boots with glory.

Okay. Sermon over, for now.

Do I have your attention?

Are you getting to a point where enough is enough; when you're tired of mediocrity, when you're worn out from the compliancy of serving and seeking the approval of others? Can you begin to lean into doing the opposite? Can you start to see the other side of your story?

The Other Side to My Story

I can pretend that being unapologetically yourself doesn't include elements of loneliness, but that would be a lie. However, if you honestly score where you currently are, can you truthfully say being misunderstood, unheard, unseen, taken for granted, or pleasing others isn't also tragically lonely? It's impossible to not—the company you keep inside your thoughts will always make you miss your authentic self if you're not true to who you are, so if you're going to experience some loneliness, you might as well at least be fulfilled.

To shift the narrative, do the opposite, and see the other side of the story, perhaps not start with the 'noise' about being rich enough to own an aeroplane but rather explore being unapologetically ordinary—to own ourselves first, before owning the money and diamonds.

However, to flip the story well, to apply the opposite, we have a few intrinsic ingredients to sprinkle in. You don't get more ordinary than a pancake; simple ingredients but utterly glorious! Like a well-flipped pancake, we need the right temperature, ingredients, and technique.

Compassion

The first condition of a well-flipped story is compassion, and that starts with compassion for oneself – by recognising you are enough. Then, we can extend that compassion to parents, siblings, teachers, peers, neighbours, abusers, oppressors, betrayers, confidence squashers, and anyone else you want to add to the list.

When Mom was a child, she was rewarded for illness somewhere along the way. She had epilepsy, and I guess she was pitied. Epilepsy was still stigmatised, and those who suffered from it were subject to the cruelty of society's judgement. It was something to be ashamed of and misunderstood.

My grandparents loved their daughter, who was clever, strong, and capable but who was afflicted with something that society didn't accept.

From all accounts, she had always been a handful—not much of a surprise—but they felt sorry for her because of epilepsy. Whatever misdemeanours or outrageous behaviour she perpetrated were always forgiven, wrapped up in pity, and overlooked out of love.

Unfortunately, this began the avalanche of a lifelong strategy of lousy behaviour, followed by illness, forgiveness, and an opportunity to manipulate and seize more power, leading to more unruly behaviour, more illness, and an endlessly vicious circle.

I wonder who she would have been without that excuse. Would it have irradicated narcissism?

Probably not.

I've told you about her unpleasant side, and I imagine you can appreciate the price those around her paid, but now I'm going to tell you the other side of the story.

My mother was nothing short of one of the most extraordinary women you would ever have met.

Her charisma and charm were hypnotic and magnetic. Her stance and persona made her stature regal.

Her beauty was beguiling, her mind extensive, and her instincts razor-sharp.

Her ability for business was mind-blowing, and she could give you a masterclass in sales, negotiation, and persuasion in her sleep.

She was feminine and masculine, both nurturer and fixer. She was always right.

She was raised by my sweet-natured nana—for whom my mom would have probably been quite a scare—and my military grandad, an SAS veteran, and my hero. He didn't discourage his offspring from spreading their wings or pigeonhole them as simple homemakers just because they were girls (my bloodline has more spirit than that) but also didn't compromise on an old-fashioned taste for what a lady should look like and walk and talk like either. To be raised as an eagle in the robes of goddesses is a beautiful concoction, as was my mother.

Mom was a 1970s middle-class middle-England housewife who was everything but that stereotype. She made it crystal clear to my dad what he could do with his Victorian expectation of what kind of wife she was going to be, and she reinforced that further through her two daughters, resolute that our gender had no bearing on what we could do. In fact, it was a bonus that we were girls—there was nothing that boys could do that we couldn't but PLENTY that girls could do that boys couldn't!

If we're going to tell ourselves we like honesty and integrity, we must include the whole truth. That means the full, unedited story, not just the narrative that keeps us in sorrow.

My mother taught me everything I needed to know, one way or another. She taught me toxic love, abuse, and neglect, and I thank her because I know what that looks like and know how to create the complete opposite.

She exposed me to the elements, and that taught me independence, fearlessness, responsibility, and accountability. It made me learn communication, expression, and creativity. It fine-tuned my instincts, and my ability to be self-reliant, and empowered me to form my own opinions and stand by them.

I know how to be practical, emotional, logistical, professional, honourable, quizzical, memorable, spiritual, and universal.

One way or another—she taught me to be unstoppable. THAT'S a phenomenal gift, and that's the other side of my story.

What if you had a less dramatic spin on your influences? That's still okay. You've still got this. You can take the lessons, look at what influences led you here and still flip the script.

Or if your history holds even more horror? Start by detaching yourself from the expectations of what childhood or marriage should look like and decide to search for the wounds of those who inflicted their pain upon you. The worse the infliction, the more aggressive the commitment to hurting you would have been—the worse was their wound. You weren't unworthy of love. You were simply collateral damage in a situation where their best was terrible, and you had no say. Being worthy is not an accurate measure, and you can have a say now.

Look at the other side of the story. Flip the pancake!
The hard truth: for every person or circumstance that inflicted you with shit, large or small, there is another version, and they will all have taught you the cream of lessons. That's the story I want to hear about. What did you LEARN? What's THAT bit of the story?
Why? Why should you give a fuck about people who have tried to hurt you? Happy, fulfilled people don't hurt others. Only wounded people do.

Yeah, I know, a fucking hard pill to swallow, but only by recognising the wounds can compassion naturally take root. Some scholars go as far as describing compassion as literally meaning 'to suffer together', but I'm not sure we quite have to go that far. Recognising it should be quite enough, thank you!

WARNING: compassion when it lands, for some, is the knockout blow. It's hard-hitting, and you can drop to the canvas when you first feel it. It's sometimes the lightning strike of the storm before the calm. Be gentle with yourself.

'Compassion' is such a great word; it is so satisfying when you roll it around your insides for a while.

Compassion – Compass - Comes Passion: the compass for finding passion for yourself, your dreams, your heart's desire, and your truth. Yes, a great word!

Acceptance

Then, through compassion, we can hold hands with acceptance. Acceptance starts with compassionate intention, not just for yourself and the people who influenced you, but also more broadly for society, secrets, sabotage, sadness, self-infliction, suffocation, sin, slights…

Acceptance is the friendly hand that reaches down and helps us up from our knees to steady ourselves again. If you crave certainty and steadiness, then acceptance is that companion; delivered not as acceptance of the shackles of compliance with other people's validation but as the certainty of accepting ourselves.

- Accepting that how you feel feels true but is only true if you believe it.
- Accepting that you can feel compassion for others—everyone is only doing their best. Even when their best is awful, it is still their best.

• Accepting that your environment is now your responsibility—utterly and wholly.

• Accepting that change makes you feel very fucking scared.

• Accepting that if you feel very fucking scared about something, that's your soul screaming that you must face it—and do it anyway.

• Accepting that those sentences that hinder you are just the bounds of your ego, which you must be compassionate for. The ego is just trying to preserve your comfort. It's just trying to protect you. It doesn't know that by doing this, it's actually causing more harm.

• Accepting that the consequence of not flipping the story is scarier than anything else that has happened to you.

• Accepting that you are a miracle: a strong, brave, beautiful miracle—an unstoppable, force with an indomitable spirit, just waiting to be set free.

Just sit for a moment with your hand in your heart, close your eyes, and revel in the possibility of compassion and acceptance; of how warm, safe, and comforting a blanket of such unconditional love feels.

How easy it would be for others to do the same if we accepted ourselves, warts and all, good and bad, happy and sad. How free we would feel with this different kind of armour on, the armour of compassion and acceptance instead of fear and lack of worth.

Kindness

Kindness is the deed of being friendly, showing respect, being generous, and being considerate. It has less sting than compassion and is breezier than acceptance—she's the cooler younger sibling, a bit more relaxed and easier going. Kindness is happy to wear relaxed sweatpants and a sloppy t-shirt. She is unburdensome and undemanding, someone with whom we can wander with little care or worry, in and out, weaving effortlessly into any nook or cranny we fancy. No permission is required.

No need to drag yourself through any blizzard, conquer any mountain, or battle through any rough terrain. Kindness is light, frisky, spring and summer.

Come on, tell the truth! Doesn't that feel good?

You're welcome!

Kindness is a funny thing, isn't it? We use the word all the time: 'Be kind to each other', 'Be kind at work', and 'Our values include kindness'. It's a word thrown around with the ease of the persona it wears, but then we forget to apply it, certainly to ourselves, let alone anyone who pisses us off.

Yet, it's so very familiar. How simple, as such a frivolous word as it is, would it be to pick up and wrap in our palms as the treasure it is? How easy would it be to pop it in our pocket? Or could we have a little nibble, savour its juice, and swallow kindness for ourselves?

We are pummelled with the word kindness as much as any other message, if not more. It's as much of us as anything else. Pick it up and put it in your pocket!

Can we share the marvellous secret that all this is already inside us? Can we go on a conservation dig to unearth ourselves? We've just buried ourselves deep underneath the sentences, thoughts, and beliefs we've stacked up. You don't need anything more than starting with enough is enough, looking for some opposites, and flipping the story.

Then comes Compassion, who passes the baton in the relay race to Acceptance, who tag teams with Kindness, who is your insurance policy to fulfilment, self-worth, self-validation and compass to your glory and freedom.

CHAPTER FOUR

Fuck You

February 1989 (ish)

My parents said their goodbyes and left after they'd helped me in with three black bin bags of belongings and my two children. They'd popped to the local shop with us to buy a few essentials we'd forgotten—toothbrushes, toothpaste, and soap. Mom told the children they were having a little holiday.

My numbness as they drove away was so substantial that I strangely felt it to my core, if feeling numbness is comprehendible. Trying to understand how they could leave us in this God-forsaken place was too much rejection and truth. Little did I realise at the time that it wasn't God-forsaken. That it was, in fact, a Godsend.

The confusion of reconciling their rejection would have probably pushed me over the edge, and I could not afford that. Not this day. I had to be strong. My children needed the bullshit, in the feeble attempt at normalising the fact they'd witnessed terror throughout the previous night, then been ripped from their home and delivered here. Yes, that made sense. Let's bullshit our way through normalising the least normal thing ever to happen to them. That was far easier than swallowing that my parents saw parenting differently.

I looked at the never-ending flooring of cheap orange lino. It's funny, isn't it? How our brain works under immense shock and stress. That it was this detail that stood out. As though my brain could only absorb the most insignificant of information. Maybe it was my concussion.

We were shown to our room. The three of us, tired, unsettled, holding hands. Obediently following the kind lady, like the helpless, homeless people we were. I didn't feel like the adult. I felt like the third child. I think I held their tiny hands for as much support as I was trying to give. Up what seemed more endless stairs with more endless orange flooring.

A small room. A window at the front and the side. Mismatched carpet, curtains, lampshade, and bedding. One single and a bunk bed. One small charity shop wardrobe and chest of drawers. A five-star rating for anyone running for their life. Safety, solace, sanctuary. Screams only in our heads, substantiation only in a statistic, self-respect only on the fucking floor.

My new situation. My two babies. My three black bags of belongings. My homelessness. My concussion. My parents returning to their large comfortable home and land. My bed, mine to lie in…

My newfound 'Women's Refuge' status. My children's newfound 'Single Parent' situation.

We were now just a statistic, an official measure of inadequacy, and helplessness, reliant upon the state. Another foolish girl. Who married a stupid guy and had children when she was barely an adult herself. Who had got herself and her babies into a pickle. Who now needed housing and belongings because she'd had to run from her own home and leave her belongings behind.

Just herself, her children, and her three black bin bags. In a secret location, with lots of orange lino and charity furniture, with other foolish women, in the same foolish situation, seeking refuge from their foolish mistakes, with their helpless children and bare essentials. Where we had to hand ourselves over as victims to receive the lifesaving handout of shelter.

That large house at the end of the street. Next to the phone box, among streets renowned for other women, who sold their bodies in exchange for money. The condoms that lay on those pavements and the curb crawlers who licked their lips and slowed their speed even though we were not for sale.

Those streets invited that attention, even while we would walk with our children. Testaments to how far we had fallen. The reality of safety and refuge to save our faces, limbs, and probably our lives—but only that. Nothing more. There were no pretty bows or frills of fancy. Just your safety. Just your life. Saved bones, stripped back to the very barest.

The Choice

Is the truth of facing the consequences of being in a horrible situation, failing yourself and your children and seeking an opportunity for a new start not better than hiding behind pride?

Is that enough? To save your life? Or is that the most important thing? Are you a fair trade for your stuff? Is your life worth relinquishing all certainty for? Is it valuable enough to let go of all self-respect—or the perception of self-respect, if we were considering the validation of others?

They are interesting proposals, aren't they? Attached to a life-threatening situation, I hear most agree, 'Yes, of course, my life would be worth it!' Yet, you don't see that truth enough to release yourself from your need for external validation now, while you are not facing a life-or-death situation.

Do you need the urgency of such adversity?

Would such a desperate situation help you to get it?

Probably.

As my wonderful late mother-in-law always said, 'Who don't hear will feel.'

Oh, Kathleen, I do miss you…

Another phenomenal woman, a glorious queen, who was mis-sold a set of hindering beliefs. Who in honour of, I implore you to listen, to hear. I pray you feel the benefits of my sentences instead of the shatter of regret in your final hours.

Is the truth of failing yourself by settling for second best not enough? Does it have to be a dramatic catalyst for your action for self?

I had twenty-four hours to choose. Choose safety? Choose life? Choose to relinquish everything to get it? Choose—stay where you are, in danger, or leave with virtually nothing and surrender to state safety and be a drain on society. That's what I had to decide. You can choose to stay where you are, comfortable and seemingly 'safe' but in danger of unfulfillment and regrets, or you can accept the risk that goes with striving for the life you want.

A single mom, barely into adulthood, with two small children to feed, state benefits, no home, no money, and no belongings. That is what I chose. I chose life.

Do you see why the word 'safe' means something different to me? You shroud yourself with your version of safety, being too afraid to come out of your comfort. To me, that's not safe. That's sacrifice. And we are all better than that.

What did I do with my new situation?

I had already mastered the Fuck You attitude. If it was possible to take an exam for this, I'd have been awarded an A-star a long time ago. Fuck you, narcissistic mother, unprotecting father, judgemental peers, who saw nothing more than the fancy house and privileged upbringing and an ungrateful, unruly child. Fuck you, school, that I'm clever and should have done better—you bored the living shit out of me. Fuck you, school friends, most of whom didn't invite me into their fold. Fuck you that I was too tall, too skinny, was late to hit adolescence and wasn't allowed out or to wear makeup or cool clothes. Fuck you that my parents had a large house and yours didn't. That isn't my fault. Fuck you for not seeing a girl who just wanted to be accepted for who she was, but who'd had to negotiate being alone pretty damn quickly and do the best she could with what she had.

I wonder why we don't ask 'Why?' more often. Why did I misbehave? The answers were all there—hardly quiet or secret. Happy people don't lash out. Frustrated, unfulfilled hurt people do…

Fuck you all, who thought you could make me comply through fear.

Fuck. You. All.

You see, there were two people, two beautiful human beings, whose wonderful contribution to my life can never be undone.

For the first three years of my life, I'd had grandparents who filled me up with so much love that nobody could touch me. Who told me that I was worth everything because I was everything to them. Then, I was thrown into the lion's den with a mother who educated me on how to hold onto those self-worth beliefs as if my life depended on them—because it did.

As does your life depend on self-worth. We're no different.

At age three, I lost Nana, although I still felt her. She'd imprinted her love within my every fibre, so leaving the physical world meant nothing because our hearts were still tied. Grandad couldn't keep me on his own, but he was still there. He may not have been local, but he too was imprinted. They had claimed me, and I knew what that kind of love felt like to the depth that not even death or distance could take away.

They taught me to love, and then life taught me to love myself. Shit or bust.

Choose Life

I chose life. I chose love, albeit a fucked-up version, but still, I was barely an adult and doing my best.

Do we get to form a Facebook group and revel in the whys and wherefores of domestic violence? To collaborate and concentrate on all those social issues?

No. Well, maybe at some point down the line. Maybe.

The same goes for childhood shit. I haven't set up a group, but I've at least changed my mind about considering it. Not to glorify the pity, only to glorify creating a better outcome. For the record, my inner Fuck You just popped up to remind me I can do that; change my mind because it's my mind to change.

Do we get to forgiveness yet? No, we get to carry on saying 'Fuck you' first!

As I deconstruct my journey, it turns out that my education in uncertainty—facing fear, choosing life, no matter the cost, in choosing love, no matter the consequence—was all I knew. Yet even though I knew not the why, how, or where and was familiar with fear and discomfort, I also knew faith and love.

I made a promise to myself when I was very young, too young to understand the magnitude of promises, I have no fucking idea how I knew to do this: I REFUSE to get old and have regrets, and I REFUSE to lose faith in either myself or mankind.

In hindsight, I can see that I had been in survival mode since I was three years old, and somehow, the love my grandparents had given me penetrated my soul and delivered a strategy. Just with those few short years, two ordinary, glorious human beings probably saved my spirit and equipped me to protect myself from when they were gone.

Thank you, Mom, for leaving me with them. Thank you from the bottom of my heart, and I wouldn't change a thing.

I'm a far cry from Mrs Fuck You now. Mostly! She still seeps through and pops in to say hello occasionally, and I'm always pleased when she does because she was my best friend for a long time, and I like her a lot!

There is always someone to get on my nerves just enough to resurrect that old familiar buddy or occasionally someone who thinks they can tell me I can't do something. However, I now know other healthier, calmer, less dramatic ways to express my irritation. Still, it really gets on my nerves that we dismiss this strategy because it's got a lot of people through many a pickle!

Revenge isn't healthy, but we must work with what we have, and if this is all we have, then we must start there.

My default advice is to talk to your heart and your belly and to listen to what they say because they have all the answers and never get it wrong. Ever. Sometimes that leads us to a bit of Fuck You, and temporarily that is a marvellous alternative. I'd recommend a short burst of Fuck You over planning vengeance. Out-and-out revenge yields far less long-term satisfaction. If flipping the script into compassion isn't plausible yet, maybe try Fuck You first, or if you're already here, let's go with it for a moment.

'Well, what the fuck are you going to do now, with your sorry arse stupid situation?' I asked myself, sitting in that room with my bewildered children, leaning into all my patheticness. Then I decided:

I am not a victim; he is more damaged than I am. I am not homeless. This is merely a sabbatical. I don't know how, but I refuse to end up in a high-rise flat with drug addicts as neighbours.

My children will not be predetermined by any socially agreed status of belonging to a single-parent home in poverty. None of this will have a single bit of influence on what they deserve. We will never be described as people who can be put into neat-and-tidy boxes.

It matters not that my parents, who could've housed me or helped me differently didn't or that they judged me. I'll sort this myself and won't owe anyone a damn thing when I do.

This situation will NOT change anything about who I am. No. And fuck anyone who tries.

Sounds fine. It did work for me. But there is a consequence, which is the start of resentment. A sprinkle of poison here and a smidgin of venom there is all it takes for the onset of a toxic infection. Watch out for that.

We settled into our room and eventually went back downstairs to gather our bearings and see who we shared a home with.

Kinship

My first introduction was faced straight away, a petite young woman in very creased clothes, who was attending to her adorable young son. She'd forgotten to grab an iron, an easy thing to overlook when running. I liked her face very much.

'Hi, I'm Dawn.'

Something about the look in her eye made me feel a kinship before we'd even exchanged a single word. When two strangers share adversity, shame, naked failure and vulnerability, there's no room for scrummaging for dignity. Words are unnecessary and ridiculous.

Our kinship was sealed all those years ago in sisterhood and a shared fuckup. Followed by the promised victory in the resolve that this was not our final story or our children's. We would be more than this without a single requirement for the validation of anyone or anything.

A lifelong friendship was born. It was no longer 'me'. It was 'we'. Two young women with three children, homeless and helpless. But instead of wallowing, we decided we would have a great time.

We went to the park, and our children played, and we sang songs and kept our tears for when the children slept, and we used our imagination to create a different mood, a different narrative.

We held each other's hands through court cases and housing meetings. We laughed at everything we could and only cried when we had to.

We had to walk everywhere, and as we did, we plotted and planned. We explored and embarked. We walked, we talked, we dreamed, and we schemed.

We laughed and laughed. And our children laughed and laughed.

Two ordinary young women. Gloriously in a pickle. Gloriously ordinary but glorious all the same. Gloriously indomitable in spirit.

Years later, another friend needed refuge, and I accompanied her to the appointment. As I waited in that reception, there were five other war-torn, tense, bedraggled women. I became conscious; conscious that I looked so very different, that they would presume I didn't know what I knew, and that my appearance might make them feel even more shit than they already felt.

The irony is that their shame was felt against failure and hopelessness while mine was for looking successful and knowing there was hope. Which is ridiculous. It was indulgent on my behalf that I could align my embarrassment with their desperation. I felt the sudden need to hide the glorious result of overcoming this same situation. But what world do we live in that tells us to be ashamed of such bravery and strength? What kind of societal pressure do we absorb not to celebrate?

I meekly pushed my stylish leather handbag out of sight. I took off my Chanel sunglasses. I wanted to scrub off my makeup. I wanted to declare that twenty years ago, 'I was you, but it'll be okay. All you must do is...'

And I stayed quiet...

Do what, Dawn? Go on, put it into a paragraph. Then, construct the road map with a simple set of directions...

While they were in the pit of adversity, when surviving minute by minute was as far as they could see, as much as they could manage...

Stay silent. Have some respect. The last thing they need is you harping on about it being okay. You'll make them feel worse!

I was so conflicted. The urge to comfort them versus the risk of making it worse was torture. Staying silent won.

When I came home, I phoned my best friend, and she understood. We cried with compassion for those women, and we soothed ourselves by congratulating each other for coming through it.

We reminded ourselves how important it is to remember, but more importantly, we remembered why we had come through. What we'd had to do. The mindset we had to develop. The promises we had to make to ourselves, why we were not going to be defined by that time, and why our children deserved more. That we wouldn't change a thing because it was part of what made us who we are. That through it all, we'd had each other.

If I were given the choice of erasing that whole time, I wouldn't because I had the very best friend in the world and just knowing her had made it all worth it. We also acknowledged that we had learned so much about ourselves, those lessons made it a valuable enough exchange.

It turned out we weren't stupid after all. On the contrary, we were marvellously brave; we threw validation away in the name of being saved because we knew we were worth more. And that is fucking inspirational.

To take it one step further, we accept the wonder of adversities and accept them as gifts. Gifts that we can receive, unpack, say thank you for, save as treasures, and then use forever. Incredible lessons to replace bullshit beliefs to pass onto our children.

Poison That Heals

I think this day resolved some of my Fuck You. It brought me down to brass tacks. I'd had enough of resentment. Finally, I saw the other side of the story. I found compassion, I accepted stuff, and I was able to rub shoulders with kindness.

But it had taken decades, so I'd be a hypocrite to pretend that my Fuck Yous weren't part of my healing, and I'd be a hypocrite not to honour yours if this is where you are. So do what you must do—just don't do it for too long and do it intending to get past it without the cost of bitterness.

The Fuck You is both a blessing and a curse. You may not have survived without it but with it, poison can build up, and while that happens, your beliefs change.

With all my heart, I beg you not to allow that poison to spread too far. It's easy to become a victim of resentment, making decisions and presenting behaviour indicative of the poisonous medicine applied to soothe hurt, inadequacies, and wounds. It seeps through organs, blood cells, and bones. It sweats through every pore and drips onto those around us.

Happy, fulfilled people don't hurt others. Happy, fulfilled people don't poison themselves. Only dissatisfied folk do that.

Your Choice

So, who do you want to be? If you could choose in the next twenty-four hours? Who do you need to apply some compassion towards? Who do you need to accept? Who do you need to be kind to? Who do you need to say 'Fuck you' to?

Top Tip: put yourself at the top of that list; you stand no chance if you don't start with yourself. Because while you're busy being Mr or Mrs Fuck You, you're also fucking yourself—IF you indulge!

You see, it's much easier to blame our circumstances or treatment from others. Of course, it's true that some of that couldn't be helped and wasn't conducted by you, and you maybe didn't deserve some of it. But how will those sentences help you? We can't change what's gone. All we can do is change what's next.

The Fuck You phase isn't wholly redundant. There is just the resentment to protect against.

I now regret not speaking to those women. For not telling them, 'Please don't give up. Your children can be okay. You can be okay.' I should've told them I couldn't tell them how, but that if they wouldn't give up on having faith... if they just had faith that somewhere deep within each of them was an indomitable spirit... just maybe hope could improve for them.

I shied away from doing that because I worried about what they would think of me. I didn't self-validate. I robbed them of seeing in the flesh a woman like them, who had come out the other end. Shame on me for putting their approval before doing the right thing.

This is the bit we don't always see. We think we are protecting ourselves, or others; however, I wonder how many times we haven't served someone because of one of our bullshit beliefs?

Good Fuck Yous

If you weren't clever enough at school—fuck them—let's look at what you are good at and go there.

If you are being told you should or shouldn't be rich—fuck them—leave them to their version of success, and you seek yours.

If you worry that people will judge you—fuck them—they're not going to make a difference in your final days.

However.

If you tell YOURSELF you're not worth it; if you're telling YOURSELF, you can't be loved, successful, or reach for your dreams, well, with as much love as I can muster…

Fuck you!

That sounds harsh, but that's what you're doing, turning your back on yourself and denying yourself the possibility of the things you want. You may be saying 'Fuck you' to yourself.

Soothe that by flipping the story and looking at what you can say thank you for.

Thank you, lonely childhood, for teaching me that I am enough.

I thank my parents for leaving me there that day. It was one of the kindest, most generous acts of parenting they ever did.

Can you imagine me being beholden to my mother for the rest of my life for giving me a home? Can you imagine the narcissistic manipulation that would have been bestowed upon my children? I can't imagine my perspective, thus my life, without those lessons. I can't imagine not having my best friend. I wouldn't have escaped anything. Instead, I'd have swapped one cage for another.

Thank you, poor man, for being so insecure that you resolved to use violence to keep me because it led me to where I am now. I wouldn't have met the love of my life, my now husband, my forever love. I wouldn't have gone on to have my other children.

I wouldn't have gone through the stuff that led to my perspective. I wouldn't have grown. I wouldn't have my other wonderful friends, my businesses, my community, my houses, my car.

I wouldn't be writing this book. I wouldn't have had my heart, my soul, not as it is. Because as it is, I am an extraordinary, ordinary person who basks in the glory of that title. I have an indomitable spirit that renders me fucking unstoppable.

So it is, for every one of them, with love, compassion, acceptance and kindness—I'm sorry for your sadness and inadequacies and for any hurt I imparted and thank you for my glorious existence and for allowing me to refuse your validation and, instead, to say, 'Fuck you! xx'

CHAPTER FIVE
The Certainty of Uncertainty

It's interesting, isn't it, how uncomfortable we are with being uncomfortable, and how resistant we are to change, when the truth is that change, along with a looming death, is the only certain thing we have.

We're born with total dependence upon other humans. Then, we gradually transform into walking, talking, and vertical objects who slowly but surely claim independence with every new thing we learn—changing, rearranging, growing, and evolving.

From gummy mouths grow teeth. Nappies are swapped for toilets. We move from liquids to solids, and crawling evolves into walking. Simultaneously, our habits change, our vocabulary expands, we explore and comprehend more of the world around us, and we learn to connect with other human beings.

Leaving our playrooms from 9 a.m. to 3 p.m. under the care of teachers, who treat our minds like elastic bands, pulling and stretching and measuring our academic capability. School and home are where we receive more criticism than anywhere and where more changes happen than we can count. Teachers change every year, and friends change more often than that sometimes.

Growing hair on different parts of our bodies, starting to bleed, body parts stiffening with no control, sweat and odour exuding.

Discovering style and sexuality, questioning the status quo, and being irritated with everything our parents say and do.

Fashion, music, trends, and language. Spring, summer, winter, and autumn.

We fall in love, but who do you know who is still in their first proper relationship? Love changes like the weather. How many people now do the job they thought they wanted when they were a kid?

I have grandchildren. One wants to be an artist, another a gypsy traveller, and the other fancies being a cheetah… there's a very good chance those things will change!

The economy is a consistent cycle; good times, a crash, high interest, improvement, low-interest rates, good times—rinse and repeat.

We reproduce other humans and raise them, dragging ourselves and them through their changes until they leave home when we must entirely re-evaluate everything again. The dynamic of family and friends is constantly changing. We start burying the older people we love, and others move on and out of our lives. We learn to live with the gaps.

Dreams and expectations are usually shattered in one way or another; divorce, complacency, betrayal, unhappiness, and dysfunction.

Then your body changes again, you age accordingly—and then die.

Your whole life is one change after another. We are literally in a constant state of flux. It makes no sense that we aren't okay with uncertainty and being uncomfortable. Instead, we tell ourselves that we hate change.

Are you even mildly amused at this? Has it prompted you to question yourself about the truth of where you really are with change? Does it highlight just how ridiculously uncertain your whole existence is?

I hope so!

Stuff That's Beyond Our Control

We can't control change. Neither can we control how others see things. Often, we can't even change how we see ourselves, so what makes anyone think we can dictate how others see us?

We see ourselves through foggy eyes, steamed with preconceptions, bullshit beliefs, and self-indulgence. Other people see themselves through the same tinted glasses. Then we all chase our tails, desperate for the approval and validation of each other, and we all impart our judgement, based on our insecurities.

Seeking change or approval from others is futile.

We manipulate each other with emotional blackmail and justify it all by explaining our beliefs. Quantifying the evidence of our life experience, most of which is probably true. But we miss out on all this other truth—the bits that don't serve our narrative, the parts that our ego protects us from, in the name of safety and consistency—without realising that's more suicidal if fulfilment was the goal.

With no control over certainty, we could walk down the street right now and get run over. It is a lifetime guarantee that people will reject us. We all fall short of a promotion or say something someone disagrees with and feel foolish for five minutes.

We could try to protect ourselves forever, but not only is that impossible to do, but the price of trying is a wasted life and a bitter end. Or we can get a grip, make friends with change, stop looking for everyone else's validation and live happily ever after.

We can find our forever love because we love ourselves, so that's easy. We can learn kindness because that is how we treat ourselves, so we recognise immediately when we aren't getting that back. We can follow our heart's desire, apply our genius, and earn £30 million from it.

Or we can be stay-at-home parents, raise remarkable human beings, or work in a supermarket and be just as fulfilled. The point is that it doesn't matter what your version of success is. Just seek it from a place of accepting change, self-love, and self-validation, and I promise you'll find it.

Stop bullshitting yourself that you hate change. You ARE change. It's the only certain thing each day brings.

You've never fitted in everywhere. Nobody has. We take the convenience of others, fulfilling a need in ourselves. I understand this sounds like a harsh, bold statement, and it has to be acknowledged that we don't do this on purpose or without genuinely liking others, but we do it all the same. And it's my pleasure to call out the bullshit.

You've always been unique. Every one of us is. You've never been approved of, not by everyone. The only people who genuinely validate you are the ones who embrace you, warts and all. Who don't try to change you. Who claim you. Exactly. As. You. Are.

But don't judge those who don't. Do you even do that for yourself?

Okay, so now we're really getting to it. If you don't accept yourself, how the fuck do you expect everyone else to?

Absolute self-sabotage! And you wonder why you sometimes get 'imposter syndrome'? Too right – you are being an imposter, but not in the way you apply that statement!

The Lies We Tell Ourselves

You don't accept yourself, then you seek the approval of others, and if you don't get it, decide that's proof that you're unworthy… and then wrap that justification up as being afraid of change.

Are you telling me that you're afraid of being foolish, with a serious face?! Let's go with that! Let's say you're right about some stuff… Yes, your bottom does look big in those jeans, and you're also a little irritating. You put people off because you're ever so slightly desperate. Sometimes, when you're overly nice, it's a bit needy and comes across as disingenuous.

We do judge you by your postcode and the school you attended, and, yes, your job is shitty and does possibly suggest you're not very clever. You're also too old for a social life. I'd definitely give up on love if I were you.

Now what? I have validated you, agreed you're right, and approved your conclusion. I agree that change shouldn't be on the table.

Does that feel better?

No, of course, it doesn't. Does it make you uncomfortable, the thought that I'm right to agree with you?

Here is the other bullshit. We believe in our negativity, then spend a lifetime seeking validation from others—until they validate our negative beliefs, when truthfully, we don't want that. What we really want is for others to disprove our own beliefs. You should feel very uncomfortable with that. And if you do, that's marvellous! Doesn't that tell you something, the fact that you don't like others to validate your negativity? Do you know it's bullshit already?

Face It Head-On, and Try a Little Fuck You

Lean into that discomfort. Sit with that tension. Now you're uncomfortable with the bits that deserve discomfort. Make friends with it because it is your friend. It's your North Star for when you're misaligned, or something isn't right. Your gut tells you everything you need to know. Always. It nudges you towards doing the opposite of what you feel comfortable with.

Or you could always accept that being ordinary means a subordinate life. How comfortable does that make you?

Please note, it would make me very happy if, right now, you said, 'Dawn, fuck you! Fuck your sentences and reverse psychology cheap shots. I am entitled to a dream, even if I don't know what it is. I am entitled. I may be ordinary, but I am glorious!'

Now, that's an excellent idea for a Facebook group. I take cheap shots, agree with all your bullshit beliefs, validate every negative bit of your self-talk, and then you can reply with a 'Fuck you.' What a fantastic idea!

Sweetheart, we are all ever-changing, uncertain blobs of living cells and bones, bumbling around, imposing generational shit on each other. Imagine an existence where we try to apply compassion, acceptance, and kindness. What massive difference would that make?

Where, with permission, we sometimes say, 'Fuck you,' and that is still okay!

Where we forego seeking comfort and certainty and look for

fulfilment and satisfaction instead?

Where we quieten our minds and smile, pleased with who we are.

Where we can see that there isn't any measure of ordinary because we are all exquisite in our own right. An existence where we bathe in the glory of that freedom, of not needing to validate anything to anyone other than ourselves.

Where we are unstoppable and indomitable.

In doing so, we would attract other wonderful people who were also perfectly satisfied with themselves—and you.

I ponder why change is not a barrier for me. All those childhood years of never knowing what mood Mom would be in on any given day, whether I would be in trouble or heralded as the golden child. I learned to adapt, pivot and counter in a split second. I had to learn this to survive.

Surviving without Much Validation?

As I moved into my teens, my peers developed much quicker than I did. The evidence of adolescence began for me at fifteen years old. Acceptance at school is much easier when you have boobs, lip gloss, and fashionable clothes, and I certainly didn't have those. Unfortunately, being an August-born child, by the time mine sprouted, it was practically time to leave school!

Survival at school and home required NOT needing the approval of others. By adulthood, I was proficient enough to pop this strategy into my back pocket firmly. Change was my friend. Validation of others, whilst still a want, was not a need.

Lose Your Goat

Make a quick list of the things that cause friction in your life.

- What gets your goat?
- What causes friction in your relationships?
- What makes you cry?
- How often do you defend yourself?
- How often do you do stuff out of obligation?
- What makes you resentful?
- What would you do if you felt no restrictions?
- Where are you disappointed?

Now take away the need for appeasing your insecurities and remove the need for looking for approval—sometimes that approval is wrapped up in your need to be right. When you call that one friend who always agrees with you, to validate your point, how about calling the other friend? You know, the one who will tell you some home truths… who loves you enough to do that.

Your goat is only gettable if you have a goat. Untie that, let it go, and wave goodbye to most of your friction and need to defend yourself. There is a massive and important caveat though. Do it from a genuine place of satisfaction, NOT defensiveness.

One of the hardest things I did was to resist the temptation to defend my opinion or actions for a whole month. Try it. It's tough! But worth it. When you upset someone, accept that you've done that—even if you disagree that they should be upset—and apologise, without explaining yourself. You don't need to change your view, just accept your difference.

Instead of arguing to persuade and change someone's mind, try to see things from their point of view. Have the intent of listening instead of being right. Don't get me wrong; I often mess up with this, but I can now recognise it and drag myself back far quicker than I used to. Also, I guarantee you, every time I have been sucked in, it was because I was not happy with myself. Happy, satisfied people don't act like that. Hurt unfilled people do.

Instead of asking what others should be doing to fill you up, ask what you should do to fill yourself up. The results are remarkable. Try it—I double dare you.

Sitting Comfortably in Discomfort

Seeking comfort is the real enemy, not discomfort. If we make friends with uncomfortable and uncertainty, a magical thing happens. It only takes a little while before those things we thought we should avoid become just as comfortable. Isn't that remarkable? And you've already done it a thousand times without really realising.

Being born was uncomfortable, catapulting out of a warm cosy womb into the cold bright world.

It was uncomfortable the first time you tried solid food. Your tongue, throat, and digestive system didn't know what to do with that.

You were uncomfortable the first time you tried to walk. You hadn't ever borne that weight before, and your balance hadn't been activated, so your legs didn't understand how to keep you upright.

We can learn so much about how miraculous we are by simply returning to our childhood and considering all the remarkable milestones we overcame while blissfully unaware of the dangers of choking or falling hard. At a stage in our development when the influences and beliefs we would inherit had yet to be absorbed entirely.

Imagine if you had all that childlike curiosity and trust now, as an adult. Who would you be if you were comfortable with being uncomfortable? What would you do differently knowing that uncertainty and change were the only certain things?

It's interesting, isn't it?

Flip the story. Do the opposite. Seek certainty in compassion, strengthen it with acceptance, and frolic with kindness. Say 'Fuck you' to whomever you need to. Make best friends with uncertainty and do it without anyone else's approval or acceptance. Instead, validate yourself because you're the only one who matters.

We suffer more without ourselves because it's very cold without the blanket of your own validation. It's cold and lonely and sad and unfulfilling. And as the chills get more severe, the soul starts to freeze. Your heart becomes hard. Resentment, bitterness, and regret become your companions.

You're better than that. You are more than that.

Indomitable from Birth

You started as a few cells globbed together. You grew yourself limbs and organs. Finally, you knew when you were ready and forced yourself through your mother's birth canal. Nothing could stop you from entering the world. You were born unstoppable, unconquerable. You were born indomitable.

You are made of the same stuff as stars; nothing is ordinary about that, my friend. Don't tell me about not being a multi-millionaire or that you do a menial job. So, what if some arsehole teacher decided you weren't clever or that maybe you didn't inherit any ambition from your parents because they were working class. What sort of measures are they anyway?

You'll have to do your own research, but it's estimated that the probability of you being born is around one in 400 trillion.[1] The calculation is based on the number of possible sperm cells that could have fertilised your mother's egg, the number of possible combinations of genes that could have resulted in your unique DNA, and a host of other factors from your father's sperm count to the time when you were conceived.

Your odds were one in 400 trillion! They're similar odds to being struck by lightning while being attacked by a shark, and they almost make winning the UK's National Lottery (45 million to one) look

---

[1] https://www.youtube.com/watch?v=Lp7E973zozc

easily achievable. Talk about uncertainty!

You are a fully-fledged miracle. The only evidence you need to justify that is that you were born against all odds, so stop your crappy stories. Officially, every single one of us is fucking gloriously extraordinary.

One other thing is certain. If you DON'T make friends with uncertainty, you are choosing unfulfillment. Forever and ever.

From Homeless to Industry Leader

My company is a national company, serving martial arts clubs, and it is the only one in the UK that does everything we do under one roof. I am the only female in the country who does my job, and I sit as a well-respected leader in my community. It's a marvellous paragraph of achievement.

How did I do this?

My husband is a martial arts instructor, and through starting a business with him in the early nineties teaching martial arts, I saw some holes in the way martial arts instructors were being supported in their businesses. It was a stereotypical 'old boy network', and unless you were in the clique, the service was shit. I decided I could do better. I didn't know how, but I listened to my heart and belly… you know this sentence by now!

In 2000, I started my business with no customers, no understanding of what it entailed or even if anyone would be brave enough to leave the fold of the old boy network and bring their custom to some woman nobody knew.

Two of my friends, Paul and Joe at Fighters Inc, ran SENI, the largest martial arts exhibition in the UK at the time, and they gave me some discounted, last-minute stand space. We threw some branded stuff together and took it to SENI at Birmingham's National Exhibition Centre (NEC) to see if anyone wanted to speak to us.

But I didn't JUST do that…

I introduced my company as the UK's leading organisation—without having a single customer—but I didn't see that as bullshit! I knew I was leading the way to a better way of doing things. Brave as fuck. Fearless. Absolute conviction. Indomitable spirit.

That bravery, fearlessness, certainty, and indomitable spirit paid off because, by year three, I could repeat that sentence, backed up by the fact that I had hundreds of customers. In an era when most women in my community were viewed as 'just' wives or girlfriends who 'helped out' with admin, and there were virtually no female students or instructors.

A black belt in martial arts had somehow become an expected qualification in our community for anyone wishing to provide services to instructors, and I didn't have one.

But I was raised by my mother—an unforgiving, unapologetic, unstoppable force who had raised us to be formidable in business and unbreakable in achieving what we wanted to strive for.

A mother who had asked me, 'If you don't love yourself, how can you expect anyone else to?' A parent that forced me to understand. Who threw me into the world with seemingly little shelter but ironically delivered the most significant protection anyone could have—the art of self-validation.

It's no shock that it didn't even occur to me that being a woman would be a problem. It certainly didn't hinder me that I wasn't an advanced martial artist—I saw all this as a bonus. All evidence showed that my peers were men who trained and taught—and were doing a shit job of looking after instructors. The only thing that occurred to me was that improving wouldn't be difficult. My inherited audacity. What a gift, right?

So, I did it, and I am still doing it.

From homeless to industry leader in a space I knew hardly anything about, and not just a male-dominated space but at the time, an anti-female one. A fine Fuck You example!

But it wouldn't be possible if I wasn't up for change. It wouldn't have been possible if I had sought the validation of others. The result impacted change in a community nationally and has helped thousands of people.

Please, stop your crappy stories, bullshit beliefs and arguments for your limitations. If your life depended on it, what would you do? How certain are you that some change isn't worth it?

Twenty-four hours. You choose.

CHAPTER SIX

The Kingdom of Bullshit and Boredom

Did anyone tell you that you bore yourself and everyone around you with your bullshit beliefs—the same sentences and worries, over and over again? And I have another question for you. If they were true sentences, why don't they apply to everyone?

I know it's comfortable for you, but isn't it a little tiring? How does it sit that others don't really want to hear it? If you have children, how good a job are you doing at inspiring them to have the same insecurities or limitations?

Imagine your daughter meets a man who is richer than you. Should you tell your daughter, 'No, honey, I know you love each other, but you're not good enough for him because we are "ordinary" people. Let that one go. He's only the love of your life. I'm sure someone who will make you quite miserable will come along instead, but it's okay because we aren't measuring worth on character or love. We are only measuring it on financial wealth.'?

How Do You Measure Extraordinary?

Or would we see that she is kind and funny and has virtually never made a bad decision; that with her feet firmly on the ground, she has morals, values and integrity? Their partnership would not be one-sided. At the very least, she brings as much to the table as he does. She brings trust, authenticity, and no ulterior motive. She brings true love. Pray tell, if that's not extraordinary, I don't know what else is, and it is priceless. This example is one of my children. My perspective is built from my philosophy.

I didn't walk out of my first marriage with two babies and three black bags without very quickly facing poverty-driven circumstances, which bring poverty-driven decisions and choices. However, I was raised by a queen. I knew how to walk like that regardless, so naturally, my answer? To walk into every room as if God himself had put me there; to take every step as if I was the wealthiest woman I know; to keep my promise to myself not to lose faith in mankind, and to make sure my babies knew how to feel wealth, even when there was no money in their single-parent, council-house-poverty circumstance.

If you don't feel your true value, maybe that's because you're measuring ordinary against wealth and external stuff perceived as extraordinary. You could measure it by your job or the size of your house... or we could flip that a little?

Instead of measuring your glory or true value on 'stuff', could we measure it on how satisfied you are, how pleasurable it is for others to be around you, and how you impact those you interact with? If you crack this bit, the 'wealth' will come, if that's what you'd like.

How bored are you? Are those sentences that hold you back boring you yet? Rinse and repeat. Rinse and repeat.

As ordinary individuals, we touch around a thousand people throughout our lives. Those people each touch another thousand, and so on, so before we know it, a billion lives are impacted.

I have helped thousands of martial arts instructors, who teach millions of students between them, who then all have families and friends. What a global, generational ripple effect. What a tragedy it would have been if I had listened to all the naysayers when I started my company.

As an ordinary person, you're already in that cycle too. You may as well make it extraordinary!

Who Do You Need to Be?

Imagine you gifted yourself with a new perspective. Imagine you swapped it for *who* you are instead of *what* you owned.

Who do you need to be to be satisfied? Who do you need to be to feel extraordinary? Who do you need to be to contribute to touching a billion people?

Maybe you also want the 'stuff', the 'financial wealth'. Your history, experiences and current circumstances aren't the reason you don't have them. It's your boring, bullshit beliefs.

I'm not saying getting wealth is easy. It's not, especially when your starting point is further back, but therein lies my point. It's *who* you need to become to overcome all that. There's no such thing as a get-rich-quick recipe, and even if there were, given your current negative self-talk, you'd likely mess it up. Success comes first from changing your beliefs and truly owning your worth.

Who do you need to be?

- Not someone who regurgitates inherited beliefs
- Not someone who passes fear forward
- Not someone who bores themselves and everyone around them by arguing for limitations

Not when it's so easy to decide another way.

In twenty-four hours, you can decide you've had enough. You can decide life.

In twenty-four hours, you could start a path of changing habits.

In twenty-four hours, you could do the least boring thing you've ever done and decide to peek around the door at how glorious you are.

- Decide that enough is enough
- Flip the story
- Hold hands with compassion, acceptance, and kindness
- Drop the Fuck You
- Make friends with change

• Choose the discomforts that bring satisfaction
• Dissolve bullshit beliefs
• Lean into faith, despite your circumstances
• Impact a billion people by impacting those thousand souls you come across
• Redefine how you think so you can secure peace in your final hours

How unstoppable do you think you would then start to become? How fucking glorious would that be?

Build a New Starting Point

Some of you may ask at this point, do we get to forgiveness yet? Nearly. First, I want you to sit quietly for a moment and imagine...

Imagine you were excited. Let that excitement waft through your body. I know you're making it up but do it anyway.

Imagine you were a child again, without all your experiences; that you could be brave enough to play at life for a moment; that you could make it up.

I realise this is weird. It feels counterintuitive when we're used to being told repeatedly to plan, be practical, work hard, and stay in our lane. But all these things are about other people's validation and fears.

I want to show you a space that, when times are hard, you can escape to. If you're going to indulge in any bullshit, this is where it's productive. This is where it starts. If we can bullshit our brain about why we can't do something, we can bullshit our brain that we can. We can bullshit ourselves into excitement and satisfaction. And you can't tell me this is shit unless you do it! Try it. Commit to it.

The brain then starts to respond differently.

We stand taller, we move differently, we have a different look in our eyes, and we start to see through the fog.

Our brain starts to search for different sentences and find different opportunities.

Our ego quietens as it doesn't feel it has to protect us so much.

Decide as if you have twenty-four hours to choose life.

I had nothing, nothing but two babies and three black bags of clothes, but I made some decisions. I asked who I needed to be.

Talk to your heart and belly and listen to what they say. They have all the answers and never get it wrong. Ever.

Slow your breathing and listen to your heart. Set the intention. Feel excited.

Don't consider the how—that's not your job.

Let the outcome go, and dive, soul-deep, into faith. Just trust.

Set your vibration. Feel genuinely satisfied.

Only ever take inspired action from a place of purity.

It hasn't been easy, but I also made it more challenging than it needed to be. If I knew then what I know now, my life wouldn't have been so bloody dramatic. The wars and battles would have been minimised. Then again, I only know what I now know because of those years, so it's all good. No regrets.

This is a testament to it never being too late. It's taken over fifty years to learn what I know, my whole life to discover some of the easier routes, but even doing things the hard way, I still achieved a lot. I have raised four magnificent children. I have found the love of my life. I have phenomenal friends. I am a leader in my professional field. I have broken some barriers. I have some of the 'stuff' too, which is lovely!

The sole reason those successes took place was the decision that I was more; the permission I gave myself, despite there being no evidence that I would be satisfied or that I already was glorious and extraordinary.

I have fewer years on this earth to go, but watch how that goes— next version, next chapter, next adventure—because I have already made the decisions.

Are You Coming?

Will you join me? We're nearly there. I'd love it if you came along.

This is a short chapter. I'm still just making the book up, chapter by chapter, sentence by sentence, word by word.

And this chapter is boring. I will stop now and finish by asking you to stop being boring too.

CHAPTER SEVEN
Glorious Gratitude

Spring, Early 1990s

I stopped at the end of the small drive. The hedge and grass needed cutting and the slabs needed sweeping. I heard myself sigh and realised I didn't own any equipment for doing those jobs. The door was wooden. The keys were in my hands. 'Come on. Let's take a look. It can't be too bad,' I muttered to myself.

After many months at the hostel, the council finally allocated a house, and by this point, I was reasonably relieved as this one was the best of a very bad bunch of unsavoury places to live.

End house; drive; front and back garden; three bedrooms; a quiet street full of families who had claimed that area for several generations. The garden backed onto a primary school. There was a small family supermarket a few minutes' walk away, a huge park, and the two local bus stops would get me to wherever I needed.

No prostitute-filled streets. No condom-filled pavements. No curb-crawler-filled roads. Sounded perfect enough for me to accept. It's funny, isn't it, how far the criteria for 'perfect' falls when you're at the bottom? Can you imagine?

'So, Dawn, what does perfect sound like?'

'A south-facing garden, no heroin-addict neighbours, and no used condoms outside the door...'

The front door opened into a tiny hallway where the stairs were and the entrance to the living room. The former residents had stuck antique gold-coloured quilted plastic to the internal doors. I hadn't ever seen anything like that. The lounge was surprisingly roomy. It housed a gas fire, which was the only source of heating in the whole house, something I didn't consider an issue until winter came, when we had to abandon our freezing bedrooms, and the three of us wrapped up together in that living room, grateful for the warmth of that ugly brown gas fire.

The kitchen was the oddest arrangement. The sink sat in a unit with a patterned blue curtain across the front. There was one other base unit with a draw and cupboard, one plug for a cooker, and that was it. To the left was a wall, behind which the fridge presumably would have to go, and another door to a downstairs toilet. The hot water tank led through to a tiny bathroom to the right, housing just a sink and bath.

It was grim as fuck.

Made for Each Other

Numbness was the nearest response. So tired. So run down. The house and I bonded that day in that mutual exchange. It looked like I felt. Maybe we needed each other. We could rejuvenate each other through the sanding of every surface and each stroke of fresh paint.

We were both empty and uncared for, opposite but the same. I looked fine on the outside, but cracks were appearing inside. This house bore its cracks proudly but was solid as a rock. I still own this home to this day. She is still going, sheltering another family who are finding their way. Who would have known all those years ago that this would be the best investment I had ever made?

I was beyond hopeless. I had come through that. My accepted shame and long-abandoned pride, with a little faith, hope, and gratitude for small mercy, were all I had left. I would put my blind faith in these walls. My babies needed a home. I needed a home.

I picked at a piece of peeling wallpaper. Then I pulled. The plaster behind it crumbled off with the paper as I did so. The same happened in the living room. 'Well, that's not great, is it?' I moaned. I looked at the stairway walls. I pulled at the wallpaper again. I brought more plaster down with it.

As I digested the reality that this depressing place was our new home, with strange quilting on all the doors, virtually no kitchen cupboards, riddled with damp, in need of plastering, and we had nothing, I became angry. *How the hell am I going to get this into anything even resembling a home?* I experienced a Fuck You moment. Fuck you, council, for your shit housing; fuck you, pathetic man who rendered me here; fuck you, parents; fuck you, world…

I sat on the kitchen countertop and cried. The tears flowed for some time. As I wiped them away and caught my reflection in the kitchen window, I promised myself, 'This is not forever.' Simultaneously, I reminded myself that, at the very least, we would be safe. For that I was grateful, and with that, gratitude became my new friend.

Standing Firm

The arduous battle to get some support for a habitable home then ensued. Sometimes you have to decide. You have to draw a line and stand firm. You have to do whatever it takes.

The council refused to let me return the keys. I refused to move in until there were at least plastered walls. The catch was that rent was due on the property. Housing benefits would not pay for me to stay in the Woman's Aid hostel and cover the rent on this property. I still wouldn't move in, and with my huge gratitude, the refuge didn't throw us out. Having somewhere to stay meant I could use the unpaid rent as collateral to put pressure on the council to fix the state of the house.

Legally, I was responsible for the rent, and letters threatening legal action started coming through, but my stance remained the same throughout: 'Of course, the rent is my responsibility, and I will move in. The sooner you make the property habitable, the sooner we'll be in, and the rent will come through.'

A court case was set. I was up to my eyeballs in back rent and being threatened that I would lose the house, still be liable and wouldn't be offered another property moving forward.

I couldn't stay at the hostel forever. You had to be on the council house list to get a housing association property, and I would never have afforded a private rental. Options seemed very limited!

But I had decided, and I did what I had to do. When you do something, with a clean heart and a determination that would scare hell, even when you don't know how to find a way, something always pops up. In my case, that something was a phenomenal charity called Shelter. They saved me. They gave me a solicitor under Legal Aid, and we got to work.

A few months later, the backlog of rent was written off, the walls were intact, and we moved into our new home. It was still grim, and I still had nothing, but we were safe. Although it wasn't much, it was our sanctuary, a place we could call home, and even though it was never really home for me, it was for my children. It was a place where, when we shut the door behind us, nobody else could get in. We were very grateful. Even in the winter, when it was so cold that we had to sleep together downstairs!

Nurturing Gratitude

There is a beautiful purple orchid called Glorious Gratitude. Go and order one. Buy it for yourself. Place it somewhere you can see it often as a living, breathing reminder to be grateful.

To free yourself from any Fuck You shackle, you must find gratitude. This is sometimes the most challenging thing for many, and as the whole 'gratitude trend' grows, the message is also just becoming part of the noise. The last thing I want to do is add to that.

Can we turn off our devices and put away the gratitude posts? Can we sideline the regurgitated vanity sentences that sound good?

Let's strip it all back and start from the beginning, not from what the gurus say, even those telling the truth. Instead, let's be human. Let's stick to the task of validating ourselves without anyone else's sentences or thoughts.

I'm more interested in YOUR thoughts, YOUR sentences…

However, what's even more interesting is how you feel.

Gratitude and forgiveness have fallen prey to surface-level spew—words that look pretty when strung together—and so many people struggle to find words. It's another barrier to entry: 'I'm crap at expressing myself. I'm rubbish at finding the words. I'm not clever enough.'

Well, good news, you guys have the advantage here! Those who are clever with words and articulate sentences often don't tap into the feeling because they assume they get it. It's not about words. It's about feeling. If we don't feel it, nothing anchors in. If we don't feel something, the words are empty.

In the last chapter, we discovered how to con our brain, and if you must do that with gratitude, please do it. Genuine gratitude will follow. Just have faith. Just start with the basics.

'I'm grateful to be alive' might be a decent start, but then sit in that. Feel grateful for life. Lean back into the terror of life's end. Explore the predicted regrets and resentment. Then remember you're alive and have choices. Ignite your insides with excitement and invite gratitude. Let it marinate in your belly. If you can take this one step further and level up to appreciation, that would be even better.

Feel your way through your bones and blood cells. Imagine you can feel life inside you. The voltage of your heart beating. The miracle of breath. How, if you cut yourself, your body heals itself. How it extracts the goodness of nourishment and expels toxins. Consider how your heart continues pumping—bub um, bub um, bub um, heartbeat after heartbeat—automatically, without you asking for it. You trust that today it's unstoppable.

You can be fearless about breathing. You are already an indomitable spirit and don't even realise it. This is why I don't look to fix anything. Nothing is broken, nothing is missing, and nothing needs adding. It's all already there. It just needs to be remembered, resurrected, and respected.

Just as an ordinary person.

An ordinary miracle—a one-in-400-trillion miracle.

Fuck me! That's extraordinary. That makes each of us glorious, simply for being born.

Does the gravity of that hit you?

Gravity is something else we take for granted; it's worthy of gratitude and a little appreciation. We get up each morning and plod through our day, and not once do we consider that it's all entirely dependent on gravity not having a glitch.

We entirely trust the universe that we won't float into space.

We trust that we won't fall off as Earth rotates around the sun.

We trust that our heart beats automatically and that the sun rises.

May I point out these are massive things to ask you to take for granted, incredible features of our lives, mostly beyond our comprehension. You trust in these phenomena, but you can't trust that you can be who you want to be. Without understanding the science behind our existence or the evidence of how and why, you accept such huge potential life-threatening trusts. Yet someone else treated you a certain way, and you accept whatever they did or said as a measure of your worth or capability as gospel?

Has it occurred to you that nobody ever told you to question gravity or your heart automatically beating, and that's why you don't worry about it?

If you were asked not to question your worth by the measure of others, would you also listen? Are you ready to stop validating yourself with the opinions of others yet? Are you starting to feel how daft some of our beliefs are?

Can you feel grateful? Appreciation?

Can you?

Can you write it down? Can you stop in between and FEEL gratitude before you list anything else?

Can you love life?

Can you love yourself?

But the big question is this: can you love others, even those you thought betrayed you?

Sweetheart, I have something else to share with you, and if you can accept it, it'll be a game changer.

Nobody betrayed you.

As a child, you were simply amongst adults who were already damaged. They didn't betray you. They were doing their best, even when their best was bad. As an adult, you're now in charge. It's your choice. Choose to affect the next generation with your inherited bullshit or stop and decide life. It's your duty to turn this around.

For those who've had horror stories, be glad of them. You're wiser than most because of it. You have more to give. You have more to be grateful for because, I promise you, surviving those stories makes you fucking unbeatable, unstoppable and extraordinary in ways others can't begin to understand.

The rest of this chapter is for you to write. This is for your feelings, tears, thoughts, gratitude, and appreciation.

I've already sprinkled some of my gratitude sentences into former chapters. Did you even notice?

If you didn't, go back over them. But find your sentences first.

What are you grateful for?

This is your chapter to write!

CHAPTER EIGHT

The Responsibility
of Responsibility

I have an intimate relationship with responsibility. I have been responsible for myself my whole life—every decision, every act. I have always had to face the consequences. Some of those have brought huge refunds and rewards, and other times, it felt like the bill was never-ending. Either way, accountability has always followed me. I could easily have wallowed in self-pity and deflection during the more challenging times or resorted to finger-pointing. I could blame my choices on an unstable relationship with Mom or a man's insecurity that drove him to use violence. Certainly, none of those things were my fault.

As I deconstruct who I am today and seek an understanding of my core strengths, taking responsibility stands out as one that has been crucial for my survival and success as a businesswoman, leader, parent, wife, and friend. In everything, there is balance. Whatever cost I have endured within the responsibility, I have had much more return on investment in the success pot. One of the biggest gifts to yourself is to take one hundred per cent responsibility for everything that happens to you moving forward. As you work this muscle, you start to make external validation redundant. This isn't anywhere near as difficult as the blame game.

We Contribute

The first step is to accept that we contribute, one way or another, to everything.

Hmmm, I hear you think, *how can that be right?*

Well, this will take a little fluidity in the application and some time to get into the spirit, and I request that you try your hardest to avoid being deliberately pedantic to prove any points. If we can light-heartedly agree on the concept, that'll do!

What does one hundred per cent responsibility mean?

Moving forward, you are responsible for your life, every outcome, emotion, relationship, and money. You take responsibility for your happiness, sadness, satisfaction, and dissatisfaction.

Regardless of your circumstances, the economic climate or who runs the country.

Irrespective of your education or your lack of support, whether you are working-class or not, rich, poor, academic, fat, thin, ugly, or beautiful.

Your self-worth is entirely your responsibility. It's a commitment from now on that you're in charge.

Who do YOU have to become to get the life you want?

What do YOU need to change for that growth?

What do YOU need to do for financial security?

How do YOU need to treat yourself and others for them to treat you the way you want?

Where do YOU need to take responsibility for contributing to becoming who YOU want to be?

When you feel betrayed, stripped back far enough, you would have betrayed yourself by ignoring red flags. Peel away the truth about your worth, and that'll be the root, not the actions of others.

When you argue, are you trying to prove a point, or are you listening to the other person to truly understand them?

Generally, are you listening? Are you paying attention?

There are plenty of people you can find to reinforce the things you know, but are you taking responsibility for paying attention to the things you DON'T know?

We are so full of the need to validate ourselves externally that we forget to shut up and pay attention.

Please, take it from me; I never did flight. I have spent decades fighting instead. Neither one allows you to really pay attention – and I say that, even as someone who has hypersensitive reflexes.

Deeper Meaning and Greater Freedom

Since I have stepped into a quieter version of myself, one that doesn't feel the need to fight so much, I've found out more about myself, the people around me and my world.

If you shut up, stop defending yourself, stop looking for external validation, and stop seeking the answers externally, you will discover everything you need to know. If you listen enough, everyone around you will tell you everything about their motivation and how you fit in. If you shut up, decide to take responsibility, listen, and pay close attention, you'll discover that you know everything yourself.

Your heart will tell you when you're happy and why. If you're uncomfortable with something, it'll tell you whether it's your ego protecting you, you're just scared because you're stepping into an unknown, or something is off. It'll tell you whether someone else has a selfish motive even though they often act unconsciously.

In this space, you develop a relationship with faith—learning to have faith in yourself. When you do that, you start to trust yourself, and somehow, this allows you to have more trust in others simply because you understand that they can't hurt you as you are the only one responsible for yourself.

Taking responsibility brings incredible meaning, and having meaning brings unimaginable freedom—to be you, to find your thoughts, your dreams, your beliefs, and to find your destiny. Accepting full responsibility boosts your ability to recognise whether you are making your decisions based on love, and immunity as you realise that you can't get into trouble with anyone. The power of sitting within the rule of being true to yourself is a far better version of freedom than being shackled by inherited beliefs and insecurity and thus making your choices based on the approval of others.

The decision to live by this rule is simple, but the application isn't always easy.

You have no idea what's possible. None of us do. If we embroil ourselves in a sheath of limiting beliefs and the reasons that hinder us, well, all we confirm is what ISN'T possible. By taking responsibility for that, you can see that your limitations come from you. They are your responsibility, so, if you're unfulfilled, it's on you. This is where the freedom is; the freedom to shake off the tragedy of being beholden and blackmailed by your current story. And remember, we must be aware of tragic stories—they always end badly!

Does it mean we can avoid all of life's tragedies? No, of course not. But it does mean we get a shot at surviving them with some sense of a well-lived life, and that's got to be worth something. Surely, it's worth more than resentment and bitterness? Surely you and I, as ordinary miracles, are worth more than that? Surely, it's worth a punt to honour that miracle, to respect our very existence? Despite the horror, despite the hurt, despite our tragedy? Is it not even more tragic to waste a life?

Truth

The second step is truth.

Being brutally honest with ourselves is so incredibly hard and monstrously brave, but oh so worth it, and you deserve no bullshit. That's how you reduce the betrayal, but it starts with not bullshitting or betraying yourself.

Is it true that I have made my life harder? Yes.

Is it true that I can be difficult? Yes.

Is it true that I have attracted unnecessary pressure? Yes.

Is it true that I have demons that rise up? Yes.

Is it true that I can still find love, security, and choices despite it all? Yes, and I did.

Is it true that all mothers are marvellous? No.

Is it true that having two children by nineteen years old destroys your chances in life? No.

Is it true that being homeless after domestic abuse is the end? No.

Is it true that a woman can't lead in a male-dominated sector? No.

Is it true that all your beliefs are true? No.

To take responsibility for the words I am writing, I'm interested in the parts of this book you don't like. I don't want to seek polite feedback. I also seek the sentences that you strongly disagreed with or felt massive resistance to. Not because I want to persuade you that you're wrong—but when we strongly react to something, I am interested in asking why. What are you irritated about, resistant to, or disagreeable to a particular aspect?

There might have also been sentences that prodded you in a way that you resonated. If so, what was being prodded? What resentment are you already building up? Where are the obligations and hindering behaviours?

Why is this my responsibility? Your thoughts aren't mine to bare, but my words are. My words. My book. My responsibility.

What questions then are your responsibility?

Is your job satisfying to you? Your marriage? Your finances? Do you like your friends? Do you like the current version of yourself?

It is all our responsibility to accept ourselves truthfully. There are great and terrible things within all of us. The good and bad are part of the journey. When we act ugly, it's usually because we're unhappy.

And thank goodness for that! We have a barometer that lets us know how unhappy we are or how unhappy someone else is.

The worse the ugliness, the worse the hurt. The kinder, more generous, and more compassionate we are, the happier we tend to be. I'm oversimplifying it, but they're the basics.

Making Things Possible

So comes the massive question, the secret to life: What makes us happy?

Firstly, acceptance that happiness isn't a possible permanent state. Pursuing that is futile and actually robs us of the opportunity for contrast, which would lead us to greater things.

However, we can pursue pockets of being happy and pursue possibility. Growth. Purpose. Being satisfied. Feeling gratitude. Loving ourselves. Loving others. Loving life—warts and all, evil and good, ugly and beautiful. We can choose how we express these things but make no bones; we are all capable of both ends of the spectrum.

This isn't about denying challenges or seeking perfection; quite the opposite. It's about being able to extract fulfilment DESPITE challenges. Despite the fuckups of either yourself or others.

Each of us is anointed, but we don't need a priest or any holy water. We are anointed just by living. We are already ordained. We do have a mission, and that mission is already divine. Clinical psychologist Jordan Peterson says you must pick up the heaviest thing you can carry (emotionally), and through that, if you can reveal the very best of yourself to the world, you will be an overwhelming force for good. That's about right as far as I see it.

The medicine to everything starts with honouring yourself first, being truthful with yourself first, and taking responsibility for yourself first.

It is urgent.

Make a covenant with yourself and see how much good you can do and how many regrets you slay. See how much bitterness falls away with ease. Feel how easy it is to disable yourself from limitations. Have faith that everything will fall into place if you relax into this. There may be bumps or even mountains, but EVERYTHING falls into place… one way or another.

My human experiment was to see how I could inspire other ordinary people to be brave. I started this book, and after writing only the first chapter, I negotiated to speak on a large stage to launch it. What could be more 'putting my money where my mouth is' than committing to speak about a book that I hadn't yet written and didn't have a structure for, as an unknown author, from a large stage that big names like Joe Wicks, Steven Bartlett, Grant Cardone and Gary Vayner Chuk have graced?

I may be an ordinary woman, but I'm also an indomitable spirit. I am a possibilitarian (yes, I created this word, which is both indulgent and evidence that I believe in possibilities), a lover of life and a 'let the chips fall' kind of girl, even risking falling flat on my face very publicly!

I instantly fell in love with this plan. What better way to show others that risks are mostly make-believe? When the freedom of relinquishing the validation of others is in play, anything is possible, even for ordinary people. Instead of nerves, I feel alive. I feel excited. I am so very pleased because I am being me in all my glory. In my belief, that is where the success is.

As the awareness of my looming book launch on a large stage started to become something to consider, and as I still had nothing prepared, I asked my husband a question: 'Knowing me, if you were to pick one topic I should speak about on a stage, in front of a large audience, what would you think I should choose?'

He thought for a moment.

'Having an indomitable spirit. For over thirty years, I have watched you do what you want when you want, however you fancy. You don't fail. If something doesn't go exactly as you plan, you pivot immediately and plough through. You're an absolute fucker sometimes. Unpredictable, unruly, uncontrollable but reliable at the same time.

You often say stuff that nobody else is willing to speak, and still, somehow, you haven't ever gotten into any trouble—despite me telling you that you'll fall flat one day! You are respected, even by people who you irritate and half the time, I genuinely wonder how because fuck knows how you do it.

You're the bravest, most fearless person I know, and nothing stops you. The amusing thing is that failure doesn't even occur to you, even when you're right on the brink of a firing line. You. Do. Not. Give. A. Fuck. Whilst that's scary for many, it's also inspirational. If someone stood before me, I could dismantle them physically, but you have me beat on bravery beyond physical fighting. You are an indomitable spirit. It'd probably be a happier world if more of us were that. That is what you should speak about.'

First, I had to pick myself up from a metaphorical faint. Blimey! He usually laughs and asks me why I'm asking him because I'll only do things my way anyway, regardless of what I am advised, so I certainly wasn't expecting all that to roll out.

Here is where the universe delivers exactly what we need sometimes. Although I hadn't captured it in those words, my book is about this. He hadn't even read a single word of it. How marvellous was that? I knew immediately in my belly that he'd nailed it, and my belly is never wrong!

Now you know where the rest of the title came from, and it's simply perfect.

With absolute ease, the title of book number one was secured, and my clarity was locked in. From there, all that remained was to soar gloriously into doing things exactly how I wanted to, with satisfaction.

When I ask you to have faith, I mean this: breathe, be vulnerable, don't seek approval, go with your guts, and trust yourself to be brave enough to be you. We are just scared, but the question is of what? It turns out it's mostly bullshit, and not only that; it's mostly not even our bullshit. It's inherited.

We shield our genius by searching for things to get offended by rather than having an open mind, listening, and paying attention. A life of truth doesn't just revolve around honesty. It also revolves around an open heart.

Imagine if you woke every day and looked the day in the eye with 'What's possible today?'

Is it your responsibility to seek truth, and openness? Yes, if you want to sit in your gloriousness.

How does self-validation tie into all this? We all look externally to fix our problems, but then we rob ourselves of the growth, confidence, and glory of fixing things ourselves.

If I fall flat on my face, it will be my responsibility, but so is my happiness. I am taking responsibility for my fulfilment by doing something that feels good, so no matter what, even if I only sell three books, it will be a success.

I often get described as strong, confident, and brave. Yes, those are probably all true, but there was a starting point, deeply steeped in adversity, that rooted those characteristics.

Was I strong to overcome adversity or was I strong because I was brave enough to face the adversity? I was three years old when my nana passed away, and I moved in permanently with a mother who didn't want me as a full-time job. Can we be so mindfully, purposefully brave at three years old? Probably not, and yet that's what panned out.

Faith

As a teenager who had become highly skilled in surviving a narcissistic mother, I knew I needed to get away. Was that strength? It was certainly confident, but how? Where did that confidence come from? At a time when nobody had effectively held my hand down any path of kindness, joy, or gratitude, that's what I did. I also got away from a dreadful situation to become a single mother in a Women's Aid hostel, with no evidence of many possibilities in choice and a huge temptation to trade all gratitude for resentment.

I wonder if we're brave enough to be a conduit for truth. Can we collectively campaign for the adoption of self-care, and independent thought, break generational beliefs and jump into a life of pure faith in search of our possibilities?

Can we make all blame redundant?

You think you're avoiding the chaos by staying within the confines of your comfort. Instead, you're creating something worse by avoiding yourself. It's no wonder you're out of sorts, not satisfied. It does not feel very glorious.

The answer firmly sits with living independently from other people's validation.

The beauty of self-faith comes to the forefront when you confidently discover that you're more often on the button when you consult yourself than when you consult others. Everything changes if we replace blame, resentment, obligation, and fear with love, joy, kindness, gratitude, and responsibility. Everything. Nobody knows enough to be a credible pessimist. When we close our minds to possibility, it closes off our genius.

My greatest asset is my refusal to lose faith in people. Who is on the side of good people? How much good can we do?

People-pleasing

But before we move further, can we talk about those lovely souls who still aren't fulfilled? Those beautiful, ordinary people—moms, dads, dinner ladies, doctors, accountants, bin men, school receptionists, company directors, whoever. Ordinary folk, who are lovely. They are kind and sweet. They foster generosity. They seem to put everyone else first. They get joy from pleasing others. There is just a small part missing.

They sometimes please everyone else to fill inner holes, using pleasing others to glue cracks within. That statement doesn't dent or diminish that they are genuinely lovely, but unless they are truly fulfilled, the brutal truth is, they people-please for approval.

Whether you see it or not, they pay heavily with their own hearts. How do we know the difference between being kind and people-pleasing? One is when we are just as confident in saying no when something isn't right for us and the other is feeling obliged all the time. And if we get brutal about this, agreeing to do things out of obligation, isn't very honest. It isn't honest to yourself, and not honest to those being 'pleased'. If you identify with this trait, you are in a massive cycle. You seek approval. Say yes, when you mean no. And although others accept your people pleasing, something tells them, right in the back of their mind, that you're disingenuous. Then your insecurity sniffs that, right in the back of your mind, which triggers your ego for protection. Your ego then shoves you straight back into people pleasing, to soothe the insecurity.

But you don't feel insecure because of a lack of worth. Others are responding to two things. How you treat yourself, and that you're not trustworthy.

We're not all people pleasers, but we all have a version of something like this, where we stoke our ego and create an unconscious cause and effect.

Let's deconstruct why people hedge the truth. It's only usually for two reasons. They either have something to hide, or they fear the consequence of being honest. Both situations impact trust, including self-trust—if you can't be honest with yourself, how can you ever trust yourself?

Pay Attention

To take responsibility, you must pay attention, and there is only one way to do that—to listen truly. Listen to yourself. Stop asking others so much. And if you are in a dispute, or feel defensive, stop and listen to the other person. Gather each other's point of view. Push aside the need to be right.

Ask the other person,

'What do you want?'
'What would you love to do?'
'Who would you love to be?'

Ask yourself the same.

The answers to all those questions are usually the truth. The truth before you inherited all those other people's beliefs. The truth before you adapted yourself and looked for love, attention, and approval.

Know Your Superpower

I'm a communicator. The biggest thing I got into trouble for at school was talking too much. If I had a penny for every time someone told me I was too opinionated for a girl, I would have been rich very young! If I had looked for approval, how many times would I have shut up, not asked the questions, not found answers that served my curiosity, and not explored a perspective?

Turns out, I should be talking and asking questions. I should be curious about people and discover perspectives. This satisfies me personally and is the reason I'm great at business. It leads me to find holes that need filling and solutions. That's my genius. I see things, that others sometimes don't. But I don't dig deeper in a clinical way. I'm the least nerdy person I know, and I hate numbers and spreadsheets. No, mine's a different kind of genius.

It's instinct. I talk to my heart and belly and listen to what they say, and you know the rest. I irritate people because I rarely get it wrong, and when I do—because I didn't listen to my heart and belly—I'm amused by that and think I'm cute for fucking up. Heads, I win; tails, I don't lose—another sprinkle of my mother's audacity. What a treasure her narcissism was!

So, what's your gift?

If you don't know, don't overthink it. Make it up. Like you did as a child before it all got squished away! Let me help you by making some things up—that are tailored to me and my needs—to show you how easy it is to play at this:

'*Today is going to be the best day I've ever had. This day will show me things that I like and things that I don't. I look forward to being playful and curious about where my heart takes me. I'm really satisfied with leaning into making things up, reinventing myself, and exploring who I am.*'

'*I'm really looking forward to peeking behind the doors in my mind, and it doesn't matter what I find. I'll know when I like it because it'll make me feel warm and happy, and I'll know when I don't like it, and I'll say hi to my ego and thank it for trying to protect me, but I'll kindly close that door and look for my heart instead. As a child, I loved being creative, reading, writing, and exploring the outdoors. My job is an office, and I know that stifles me, but I'm grateful as it pays the bills and feeds us, and it's given me the contrast, so I know that's not my heart's desire. As I sit here, I'm just really falling into how I feel in the outdoors, how free I feel, how full I feel—oh, I'm so satisfied right now...*'

Try making something up to suit you, and your heart will start leading you into some action but not any old action. It will lead you to inspired action!

Slow your breathing and listen to your heart. Set the intention. Feel the outcome.

Don't consider the how—that's not your job.

Let the outcome go and dive, soul-deep, into faith. Just trust.
Set your vibration. Feel genuinely satisfied.

Only ever take inspired action from a place of purity.

Turn off the news. Put down the papers. Don't be influenced by other views on social media. Instead, revel in your imagination. Bask in uncertainty. Make best friends with change. See where uncertainty takes you. See where your heart takes you.

Success isn't something that you 'get'. It's something within you that you 'do' by doing everything you want to do as well as you can. The comfort zone is the killer of success. It murders who you really are, and you are not helpless. The truth is, you're the main accomplice. Take responsibility for that and stop.

Laziness is the other culprit. Lazy in mind, lazy in truth, and lazy in responsibility. Lazy in comfort, and lazy in beliefs. Stop it. You're better than that. Once you're true to yourself, you'll see motivation resurrect.

Also, you don't have to defeat others. You can let them be. You can recognise where they are. It's how you treat yourself and treat others. It's not a competition. It's a collaboration, but it starts with you. You must collaborate first with yourself.

I have had to take responsibility since I was three years old. It's a diet that has fed my demon of feeling I have to do everything myself. My relationship with responsibility is a little extreme. My trust in myself is so solid that it's difficult for others to penetrate.

My saving grace has been that promise I made to myself as a small child, my refusal to lose faith in mankind, combined with my unshakable self-trust and ability to take responsibility for everything. There has also always been an openness of heart, which will continue unless I decide to close it.

Absolute Honesty—Full Disclosure

Taking full responsibility and being brutally truthful makes me a nightmare, especially if I close my heart to someone or let my demons rise. Walls go up. War paint applied. Weapons sharpened.

You need to be ready. If you want to beat me, you'd better be prepared to kill me because I will never give up. I put on concrete boots that are so deeply planted I become unmovable. I gather my blood cells, bones, spirit, and every fibre within my soul and set them alight, and I'll burn every bridge. I can do that because I haven't got anything to lose. I have myself and that's enough.

I can switch to that weaponised mode in an instant. If you're lucky, you're in eyeshot, and the look in my eye will be enough for you to know whether you have the belly for my wrath. Words will quickly follow, and I don't care whether you heed them or not. Whatever happens will be your responsibility based on your choices. My actions will depend on what you do, and I am comfortable taking responsibility for whatever I do.

If you're fortuitous, you'll know it's coming. You may get a chance to call a truce. However, if you've cut me deep, my response will become a stealth mission, a military operation. You need to remember that not only am I a highly trained operative at survival, but I was also raised by a woman who was a master motherfucker. I may choose not to use those skills often, but I know them, so I can easily recognise enemy territory. I lived with it, fought it, and beat it many times; and that was against my mother, my kin, so others stand no deliverance.

If you try to rob my dream, I will become your worst nightmare. If you try to fuck with me, I'll fuck you back so hard, you will want to flee to the mountains to live a virgin life for recovery. The downside to my finely tuned ability to have so much self-belief is that I'll take responsibility for all the consequences—even the bad ones, even the ones born from the wars I start.

There have been worse times when nobody was robbing my dreams, but I was so misaligned that I sat with inner anger and unhappiness. That is when my poor children or husband or anyone near me may have had all this hurled at them. Ugly sentences. Ugly truths, with little kindness… but here we are, taking responsibility and telling the truth.

I could omit these confessions to retain your affection and approval, but I would like you to stop here for a moment and pay some attention. Do you like me any less? Will you put down this book and cast me from your life because of my ugliness?

Maybe. Or maybe you can see that we are all human beings doing our best, even when it's unsavoury. Maybe you and I connect more through my honesty. Maybe if you recognise that my truth hasn't made you condemn me, you'll be inspired to have a go at your truth. Warts and all.

For those casting me aside with a swipe of judgement, I wish you well. I'm sorry for contributing to that action, and you have my compassion. I accept your judgement and look kindly upon you… because only hurt, unhappy people are so judgemental.

Youth keeps a supply of the energy you need to be able to fight the Fuck You fight. I didn't know that those battle scars start to chip away at you as you get older, and in the true sense of my philosophy, that's my responsibility. It's on me. I can try to blame people's antics, some economic catastrophe or whatever else was going on, but how I respond is mine to swallow. I mostly find a quieter version of war now.

A Softer Fight

For those who don't naturally fight, they avoid conflict instead. If that sounds like you, sweetheart, you are still in a war but more of a war within yourself. You've actually picked the more arduous battle. Your tactic is more damaging and more disruptive. That internalisation and avoidance heaps more hardships on your heart and soul, so this next bit is for you.

If you'd asked me thirty years ago, all I would have had for you was to fight in a way that, as an 'avoider of conflict', you would never have been able to consider. Now there is a wiser version, where confronting others isn't the first step.

First, you have to confront yourself a little, and yes, with honesty but equally with love. It seeks a more peaceful strategy, one that stems from compassion, acceptance, and kindness; and here is the beautiful truth: if you think I was scary in fight mode, that's nothing compared to the 'power of love' mode.

To be a sophisticated survivor, an unconquerable unit, to reign relentlessly victorious, fighting with an armour of faith, a sword of love, and a shield of truth, oh let me promise you, your indomitable spirit rises in a way you never thought possible. You don't need to get biblical if it's not your thing, but honestly, that helmet of salvation sits smack in the middle of this.

If you decide to take responsibility for your heart, your dreams, and your soul, you might have some spring cleaning to do. You'll need to throw away those outdated beliefs, give your insides a good scrub with compassion, and then you can put everything back in again but this time with order.

Who do you need to say sorry to? Do you need to start with an apology to yourself?

If you can call everyone you're close to, including anyone that has hurt you, and say, 'I'm sorry for any hurt I caused you and for my contribution,' and be able to do that in the spirit of seeking nothing back, neither forgiveness nor reciprocation, an interesting thing will follow. The connection with those who are for good in your life will deepen. For those who need to go, this will help you free them but more importantly, free yourself.

You might feel like a dick saying it to your spouse, children, or friends. You will experience powerful resistance and defiance while saying it to someone who hurt you, but remember, if you come from a place of love, you can't get into any trouble, and you have no reason to defend yourself.

I promise you this is a marvellous thing to do.

Responsibility. Truth.

As you take your last breath, you'll be extremely pleased with yourself, having lived a life well lived.

CHAPTER NINE
Forgive Us Our Trespasses

I am so very proud of you, and I don't even care if you've not managed to do a single thing—your willingness to strap yourself in and join me for the journey of exploration is enough for me. After exploring compassion, acceptance, kindness, defiance (remember Fuck You), comfort in discomfort, cutting the bullshit, gratitude, and taking responsibility, we finally get to forgiveness.

It's so annoying, isn't it? It feels so much more satisfying to hold on to the grudge, justify our indignance, and qualify our victimhood. Judging the other person reinforces our belief that we have the moral high ground; that we are a good person and the other is bad.

We love a label—'I'm good. You're bad.'

We tell ourselves, 'I am so full of goodness and such an advocate of kindness, unconditional love, and entitlement of forgiveness,' but truthfully, I pick and choose when that applies. Don't we all? Hmmm, not so unconditional.

I often advocate forgiveness when I have messed up. There's always a reason when I cause hurt, and I want to be forgiven, but when I am on the other end of the stick, and someone hurts me, I'm not quite as good at agreeing with the entitlement… Hmmm, not so good.

I have sentences, long stories of the woes inflicted upon me. Do I have to let those go? Does that make those people less horrid? Do they deserve my forgiveness? Do I want to release that indulgence? No. Not always. Hmmm, not so kind.

I am being a little pedantic here, so smile and be light-hearted about these last paragraphs because we aren't taught this skill. It's hard to forgive, mostly because of our conditioning, so be gentle with yourself.

We are conditioned to believe that forgiveness is hard. We have generational beliefs around it and an ego, whose sole job is to protect us, that hasn't evolved in thousands of years. It still responds in the way it did when we were cavemen, grunting and simply figuring out the survival of humanity, so we're definitely on the back foot!

What's 'good' anyway?

Could we look at what modern society deems as 'good character' and whether this aligns with WHO we want to be, so we at least know we are starting the roadmap for success and apply that alongside forgiveness?

According to certified life coach and published author Sherri Gordon in a published article on verywellmind.com[2], there are twenty-four 'positive character traits', which fall into six classes: wisdom, courage, humanity, justice, temperance, and transcendence.

The first five of these classes are self-explanatory. For example, wisdom includes traits you'd expect to find such as 'curiosity', 'love of learning', and 'open-mindedness'; and temperance covers 'forgiveness', 'modesty', 'prudence', and 'self-regulation'. 'Appreciation of beauty', 'gratitude', 'hope', 'humour' and 'religiousness' all come under the umbrella of transcendence.

In 'The 6 Essential Traits of Good Character, according to Jim Rohn'[3], published in the online magazine *Success*[4], the key ingredients are integrity, honesty, loyalty, self-sacrifice, accountability, and self-control. These are mostly self-explanatory, but he sums up the last trait as 'the ability to make good decisions', which is a powerful way of looking at self-control. Where we end up, what we do, what we say, what we lean into, and what we avoid all come down to decisions in

---

[2] https://www.verywellmind.com/what-are-character-strengths-4843090
[3] https://www.success.com/rohn-6-essential-traits-of-good-character/
[4] https://www.success.com/

the end. Life is a continuous process of moment-to-moment decision-making.

Jim Rohn has perfectly captured my perspective on good business and leadership. These are also the principles that my dad lived by, certainly in friendship and business—I recognise his influence there and credit him as a man of good character. Things may have got a little blurred when it came to him sticking up for Mom, but here we are, trudging through the things we have to forgive people for.

How many do you align with? Are you of 'good' character? If we should even be segmenting as good or bad, that is, but that is a contemplation for another day!

What about someone's character weaknesses? Self-deprecation, self-destruction, martyrdom, stubbornness, greed, arrogance, and impatience—notice how these ALL stem from the ego protecting us from something or other. If you own some of these behaviours, you can at least now recognise them and ask yourself what embedded belief your ego is trying to protect you from. If you consider that good character is important to you.

If this is important to you, I guess the question would be, do you want to trade good character by responding 'badly'?

Other character weaknesses include excessive pride, arrogance, misplaced trust, excessive curiosity, lack of self-control, laziness, and deceptiveness. Believing honesty is a good character trait, being brutal in truth isn't always kind! Check your ego and identify what has provoked that brutality. If it's not pure love, and you're simply trying to prove a point, then it's a weakness in character.

With all the love and kindness that I can summon—I need to be brutally honest with you—being anxious, paranoid, naïve, and too nice are also character weaknesses.

Full disclosure: I have been every single one of those characters at some point. I may have dealt with many of them, fought them off, buried them deep and tried to banish them from ever resurrecting again. However, I am human, right? Of course, we all have weaknesses.

It's what you want to do about them that counts. It's WHO you want to be, and what will be successful for you, and it doesn't have to be all the time. Just striving to develop a strength in good character most of the time is enough.

What's Forgiveness?

Psychologists generally define forgiveness as a deliberate decision to release feelings of resentment or vengeance toward a person or group who has caused you harm, regardless of whether they deserve forgiveness, 'deserved or not' being another debatable aspect. Is your character strong enough to forgive? Maybe. Maybe not, so I'll push on to drive the point home.

Resentment is the terrible price we pay for clinging to grudges or seeking revenge. Being vengeful is a painful emotion, and holding onto it makes the injustice of the incidents you endured linger in the mind, sapping your ability to find peace and happiness. Resentment then starts to infiltrate your body, spreading chemicals of aches, and inflammation, inviting disease. Disease, dis–ease, not at ease, no ease with self, equates to being disconnected from self. An interesting contemplation.

Often, we need to exonerate ourselves first, wiping the slate entirely clean and starting the relationship with ourselves again. Forgive yourself. Then we must figure out who to forgive and how we can forgive them. If they are sorry or didn't mean to hurt us and the relationship is salvageable, exonerating them can be easy.

Tread carefully through this next bit, especially if your belief supports unconditional love. Far be it for me to call hypocrisy, but if you don't feel comfortable with that accusation, be warned that we are about to dive into our 'conditions' and expose our delusion about those.

If those who have wronged us only partially take responsibility and you're a bit wary, forgive, yes, but don't forget—keep your eye out for repercussions. That's an understandable course of action, but don't con yourself; this is conditional, therefore not entire forgiveness. While watching them, you still sit in suspicion, remain in protective mode, and your ego is full-blown.

If there is repeat behaviour, forgive and get rid of them, but you do have to forgive them. Parting ways isn't enough long term. Otherwise, resentment still infiltrates, and whilst you may have removed that person, that residual energy that remains within unforgiveness will influence other relationships because your character still sits in suspicion. It raises the belief that people will hurt you, and that belief will impact some of your decisions. While we're here, can we look at this myth that we can protect ourselves forever from being hurt? This is absolute bullshit.

You will never see the world in exactly the same way as anyone else, and vice versa, and some of those differences in perspective will impact how we treat each other, so we will always have to deal with this. Equally, despite how 'good' you are, you will always hurt others, even if it's not on purpose. Can we get rid of this ridiculous expectation? Instead, maybe take responsibility that we all hurt each other based on differences in character and how we believe we should treat each other.

Then, of course, there is the hardest forgiveness—those who hurt you deliberately and take no responsibility or don't care. This will be where your sentences justifying hate and vengeance will crank up. Suppose you want to be of good character. If you want peace, you must release that.

Release sits amongst forgiveness. This asks that instead of defining your life in terms of the hurt done to you, you release your bad feelings and preoccupation with the negative things that have happened. It does not exonerate the offender.

When Mom was still here, I only managed a version of forgiveness. I know that because I could only feel forgiving from afar. Still, it became virtually impossible whenever she would poke me again with a new offence or whenever I was in the same vicinity as her. Hmmm... not quite forgiveness.

We do our best with what we can. However, I know this much: the release doesn't demand you continue the relationship to release the blame. It simply allows you to let go of the burden of settling the bill on the tax your soul is paying. You might even get a shock around this. If you take complete responsibility, you might even discover that you must forgive yourself more than you realised.

Acknowledge the Part You Played

What responsibility do you have for yourself? Have some of your beliefs around your worthiness delivered you into toxic situations? Have you sabotaged yourself? Is it easier to blame the wrongdoings of others than to have an honest conversation about your beliefs and their impact?

A classic example is the cheating partner—are they betraying you any more than you betray yourself for staying? Is the belief that you're not worthy of being treated better not a betrayal of yourself? Some of our hurt from others is on us and our decisions.

Forgiving the Unforgivable

Let's get a little more sinister—the sexual assault, the beating, the lies, the manipulation, or even the murder of a loved one. Much harder to forgive but the worse the crime, the more requirement for forgiveness—for YOUR recovery. Forgiving yourself is VERY important.

Did you do your best, even if it was shit? Did your perpetrator do their best, even if it was shit? You may feel anger. Anger and forgiveness work together often, so just be compassionate with yourself, accept that it's part of your growth, and be kind—success and freedom are on the way! If we are of good character, we could consider also making compassion available towards those who have hurt us. Happy people don't hurt others deliberately. Damaged, hurt people do. The way they treated you is evidence of their hurt, as is how you treat yourself by accepting it. Compassion—compassion for you and compassion for them.

Regardless of whoever has hurt you, whatever they did, and however they betrayed you, forgiveness is freedom of self. That's where we want to be. We want to make an intentional decision to let go of resentment and anger.

Forgiveness is a strength of good character, and it delivers a pardon for yourself. You should feel proud for even being willing to look at forgiveness because that tells you that you are an amazing person but do it for your clemency and your grace; this lights the path for you to be free of emotional baggage. Being free helps you to let go of constantly seeking the approval of others, which leads you to blossom.

An indomitable spirit is essential for success. Otherwise, you succumb to the pressures of life. Indomitability means you cannot be subdued or overcome, that you are unstoppable. It doesn't mean there won't be challenges, but that you are unstoppable in the face of those challenges. Forgiveness is one of those challenges. It is also glorious.

Deciding enough is enough, compassion, acceptance, kindness, making friends with change and uncertainty, gratitude, taking responsibility and forgiveness will resurrect your indomitable spirit. This is where Fuck You can come in very useful because you can pick that tool up as and when, without paying with resentment. However, that tactic is rarely required once you get the knack of forgiveness.

A magical thing happens when we move without protecting ourselves. I'm not talking about extreme situations, but generally, by applying this philosophy, we stop limiting ourselves, and then we are certainly well on the road to fulfilment.

And here is the final cherry...

Becoming a Force for Good

All the years you have spent seeking the validation and approval of others—any dreams and wishes not fulfilled, all that protection you gave yourself, those sentences, those beliefs, anything you blame others or your circumstances for, your upbringing, your finances, your education, your age, any resentment you're building up—and you are still not fulfilled, neither with your inner needs nor with the need for approval or admiration. None of that works, so why not try another way? We have nothing to lose.

In becoming unafraid to share ideas and thoughts, regardless of what others think, in being unapologetic about being ourselves, for standing on truth and standing up for each other, and in putting forgiveness in the pot, we're strong enough to do good for the welfare of others in a way that people pleasing never manages. You will get all the approval and admiration you need (or hopefully don't need anymore) because you will be an inspiration—an indomitable spirit, a gloriously ordinary person.

My inheritance from my mother was an indomitable spirit. She passed that down to me as I am passing it to my children and grandchildren. In that, we will have a shared legacy.

She didn't always use it for good, but I do. My job is to break that curse. You can do that too. Wouldn't that be the most satisfying, fulfilling legacy? Is a human collaboration in unapologetically being a force for good, a force for happiness and wholeness not the most fulfilling, joyous thing?

Many great films explore the theme of people sticking their necks out against the odds and overcoming adversity and challenges. We relate to feeling like the underdog, fighting against the odds, and the feeling that as the 'good' guys fighting the 'good' fight, we are in the minority. However, as ordinary people, there's an interesting perspective that we often overlook. There are more good people than bad in this world. Look for it, pay attention, and carefully observe.

Millions of ordinary good people!

As the 'ordinary' people, we are not less capable or powerful. We just don't believe we can make a difference. We have subscribed to colonisation, but it's not the 'rich and powerful' people's fault. They are very few and far between. It's our responsibility. Our minds have become colonised with beliefs and ideas that are not serving us. We really should stop that.

Instead of consuming noise on social media about getting rich quickly, let's start here, with ourselves and our beliefs, and adopt a mindset of possibilitarianism. I'm starting to love this new word of mine. Perhaps I should capitalise it and register it as a trademark. I would like as many people as possible to become possibilitarians.

What would we be without the need for the validation of others? What would ordinary mean then?

Suppose we can accept that most fears aren't true. In that case, we can explore the possibility that ordinary people could step out of hopelessness and reliance on approval. If a minority of bad people and bullshit beliefs causing unfounded fears to have had so much influence, imagine if the majority joined a revolution for being unstoppable? Can you imagine the rise in human victory? Can you feel the impact on future generations?

One day, it's possible that one of your future relatives will have to forgive you. Maybe even years after you've passed. It may be that your great-great-grandchild might trip upon their inherited beliefs and attribute them to you. They may calculate the cost of unfulfillment and conclude, for example, *'My mother died unfulfilled, but it's not her fault. It was the beliefs she was raised with. It's how her parents and grandparents lived, but I forgive them.'* That's you they are forgiving, by the way.

Doesn't that thought make you twitch, if preservation of good character is the task? Isn't that a more terrifying prospect than change? As an ordinary person, is it not viable for you to at least gift future generations with further good character? What good can they do in the world? Is this not the very definition of richness? I wonder how fulfilled and satisfied you would be on your deathbed with this knowledge.

Feels pretty wonderful to me. Forgiveness feels like a worthy exchange. If mankind has achieved all we have under such oppressive conditions that fear delivers, imagine what a world we'd create with the bravery to be all we could be. Who do you want to be? What kind of ending do you want yours to be? What will your legacy be? Who must you be to impart a world you want your grandchildren to live in?

How many unhelpful, untrue beliefs can you erase? What generational beliefs can you gift to yourself and those around you? Pick your battle—fight for love or fight for limitations.

I am a well-battled warrior and a fine-tuned strategist of survival. When it comes to my deathbed, I promise you, my battles will have been easier in the end than other people's plight for avoidance. I will have lived a life well lived, and I will have decades behind me, where apologies were said there and then, not rushed at the end out of panic. My heart will have peace as regrets will be few and insignificant. Before that day comes, I want to be a force for good and stand shoulder-to-shoulder with my faith in mankind.

I implore you to ask yourself your hard questions, to be brave enough to face the hard-hitting stuff, and then to go on to have your spirit rise and for you to be secure in the satisfaction of your final hours. What do you choose? A satisfied life, an incredible legacy; or, at best, an unfulfilled end; at worst, a bitter resentful death.

It took death for me to finally forgive my mother. I could easily have fallen into a romantic rabbit hole of wondering what our relationship would have been had I been able to forgive her before. Would it have been better? Probably not. Would I have saved myself some of the hurt? Yes, maybe, not because she stopped her behaviour, but because I had released it. Do I regret not doing it sooner? No, because we only know what we know when we know it.

I quite like her in death. I've managed to make friends with her. You know when we ponder what we would do to bring someone back? I wouldn't choose to bring her back. That is an unpalatable sentence, but this book isn't being written to seek your approval, so I will lead by example and speak my truth, even in the less pretty sentences.

The energy we sit in now is calm, and I like it. I am one hundred per cent safe. She is one hundred per cent forgiven. There is no fight or flight. I have space to remember her brilliance. It's no longer tainted with anger towards her. I have remembered some of the good things long forgotten through the spoils of our war, and I very much like that. I have been able to start grieving as an ordinary daughter, with normal feelings about being sad that her mom died—and reconciling all that with some balanced perspective.

Our family has lost several people over the last two years. This will continue as we move into this era of people reaching their time, or in my sister-in-law's case, seemingly taken too soon. This has been recent. She lost her battle with cancer earlier this year, 5 April 2023, aged sixty-one. At sixty, she still played rugby, so this was an ordinary woman who was glorious!

Our loss of her is still raw, but by going through some of what I have written about in these chapters, I am slowly becoming friends with death.

Listen to your heart…

Forgive me for not loving myself enough to release my resentment of those who have wronged me. Please deliver me the self-worth, self-care, and self-love to release it all. Regardless of what or who, give me the love for myself, to strive to forgive those who have trespassed against me.

CHAPTER TEN
Indomitable Spirit

Kathleen, my mother-in-law, had many sayings, a common one being 'Wanty wanty, no getty. Getty getty, no wanty.' In other words, if we desperately want something, we don't get it, and often, when we do get something, we're not bothered and move on.

We covet things others have. We yearn for stuff. We sell bits of our soul in the name of 'working for something'. We then revel in the glory of satisfaction, particularly if our family, friends, and peers admire and approve of us. Often, it then becomes normalised. We take that small win, relationship, friendship, or whatever it was, for granted. Truthfully, we take too much of what we have for granted. Mostly, though, we take TIME for granted. Our time left on this earth to plod along, wanty wanting... we bunny hop from one external need to another.

Kathleen lived a long life, leaving a huge family line, but despite her strength and stature, and undeniable indomitability, she didn't use any of those eighty-seven years for her dreams. She didn't know that her inherited beliefs weren't real. It's the saddest story I know. As I move into an era where we are regularly starting to bury elders, I can't dishonour their lessons by ignoring mortality.

So, what now? I can only write the sentences that my heart releases. This is my 'what now'.

I'm bored shitless. I have grafted for decades, raising a family, and taking opportunities that have been sought out circumstantially. If we park how successful those have been, NONE of the businesses were born from my heart's desire. Here I am, fifty-six years old as I write this chapter.

This is what I am going to do:

I will write a book every year until I have run out of things to say.

I will stand on stage, not sell anything, and talk about being glorious.

I will have total faith that I can start a fucking revolution to redefine what being an ordinary person is because nobody is too ordinary. Nobody. I am bored of witnessing hopelessness, listening to all the 'noise' and the 'serve' narrative.

Fuck it. My demon is that I must do everything myself, so, okay then, I'll do this too: I will get up. I WILL GET UP. I don't know how I will do it or what it will look like, but I know WHY. I will get up and…

Do. What. Makes. Me. Satisfied.

I will prove that every single one of us is extraordinary.

Only I'm not alone, not this time—because there are millions of us.

I think about some of the phenomenal men and women in my life who haven't slithered into the chapters in this book. Looking around, you'll find examples of brilliant minds, all 'ordinary' folk. Still, when you scratch the surface, the evidence of how extraordinary they are easily floats up. You are also one of those souls. I trust that makes you feel gratitude and pride to belong to such an incredible band of ordinary men and women.

Capturing your indomitable spirit starts with relinquishing the need for external validation. The only approval you need is your own. I am putting my money where my mouth is and doing exactly this.

I have written this book intuitively, word by word, sentence by sentence, at the risk of making a complete fool of myself. I am committed to speaking on a large stage for the next five years. The first appearance is in a few months—and I still don't exactly know what I'm doing.

But it still makes me happy. I would rather open this door, not knowing where it will lead, than reach the end of my days with the regret of 'what if…'

By putting into print some stuff within my heart that I have no idea whether I can pull off, I am the most vulnerable I could ever be. Hopefully, that inspires you, but you don't have to go public. All you need to do is make a covenant with yourself privately.

Let's play and see what happens. You can connect with me on social media if you're curious about this ridiculous human experiment and if you're even mildly interested in where my heart will take me—or want to see if I will fall flat on my face!

If I do fall, that will still be okay. I was raised by my glorious mother, who left me the gift of audacity. My response will be to giggle, shrug my shoulders, and tell you once again how cute I am when I fuck up. And your inspiration? That won't be compromised, as you will see how easy survival of a failure is, and at least you may then be brave enough to replace fear with action.

Except none of this will ever be a fuckup. I am writing and exploring, first and foremost, for me. So, whether anyone else cares for this or not, it's still a win. This, my friend, is the freedom of relinquishing the validation of others.

I would love you to connect with me. Let me know what you liked and what you didn't. Share your wins and challenges. Maybe we will create a Facebook group. Maybe…

Monday, 21 August 2023

The editor has just finished editing Chapter 8. He knows I have taken this final chapter out—something was missing from it, but I didn't know what. I promised him completion last week, but it didn't come to me.

Here is where your gut and heart are never wrong because who knew that the last few days would go as they did? This book couldn't have had a more profound ending, even if I had tried.

I don't know anything about publishing a book, so I have started investigating, and I don't have the budget to pay someone else to do it all and to do the marketing. The big event is in November, but I am at a smaller event first in September. I haven't finished this last chapter, and I have deadlines for branding stuff. I must submit the slides, talk title, description, and notes by Monday, 28 August. I don't have any of it.

All I have is a feeling. If you asked me to stand up on a large stage and talk about business stuff, I could do that in my sleep, but somehow, this feels very different, and I can't find the 'message' in a way that translates from manuscript to stage.

I have had several conversations with respected, trusted professionals today to unravel the mental block. Judging from their responses, it feels like they mostly think I sound delusional. You see, here is the trouble. I'm not afraid to say what I want to happen because it's too big. Quite the opposite; I'm terrified that I will not fulfil myself in a way that's big enough, but that's not how others think.

Tuesday, 22 August 2023

I have a session with my mentor, Shari. She is a kindred spirit, a maverick sister, and I will employ her services forever. With the click of a Zoom link, her happy face appears on my screen, and I tell her that I'm stuck, misunderstood, and have looming deadlines for things that I haven't got. The tears begin to roll, and something interesting happens. My tears are falling harder because I want my mom.

Mom would have looked me in the eye and agreed wholeheartedly, despite my successes, that I was right. There was more. I had played smaller than what she raised her daughter to be. There was nothing impressive about me writing a book to kickstart a revolution and sharing a stage with Mo Gawdit and Fearne Cotton because that's exactly where I should be—she would expect nothing less. In fact, she'd view this as a barely acceptable starting point. It would have made perfect sense to her.

She would have touched my arm, looked me in the eyes, and demanded my best. I was her daughter, and that was nothing short of extraordinary, and I should not let something as ridiculous as budget or a mental block or other people assuming I was scared and needed my hand held even start to penetrate. She would have found that insulting. She would have said, 'You'll figure it out, you always do, and you will do it your way, regardless of what anyone tells you.'

It was the first time I had cried like that about Mom since she had died. Like the angel that Shari is, she channelled the rest of the words I needed.

Twenty-four hours later, I had clarity, a framework, some solutions, and peace. In twenty-four hours, my mother's compassion, acceptance, and kindness saturated me. I flipped the story and said, 'Fuck you' to the frustration. I forgave her, and I forgave myself. I felt my mother's love, and I loved her back.

Thursday, 24 August 2023

I am crying as I type, but this time, these are tears of joy as I close my final chapter and make my final request:

There's no sales pitch here, no service or product that I want you to buy. I want much more. I want your heart, but I don't want you to give it to me. I want you to give your heart to yourself. Find your heart's desire and explore what it says without all the bullshit beliefs. Stand tall in all your ordinariness, break generational curses, and replace them with legacies.

I also want to thank you for reading this book, which is the art of my heart. It is an honour to share myself with you.

From this day forth, I want you pledge to be an indomitable spirit.

Because we may be ordinary folk, but within that, we are fucking glorious.

I'd love to send you a Daily Dawn, a love note to start each new day, and to connect and communicate on social media. I can wait to hear your thoughts! Simply scan the QR code below or visit dawnwillock.com

Acknowledgements

There are specific people who helped me in times of need and others who have simply been integral to this journey. It's just the right thing to do to include them in the pages of this book somewhere!

Nick James—CEO Expert Empires. For being a fine example of indomitability!

Martin Morrison—A leading ghostwriter, including for Sunday Times bestselling authors and my editor. Get the whiskey out. We've survived!

Heidi Williams—Sales copywriter. I'm sorry / Thank you / Yes / No / I don't know / You're a genius / It'll be fine! Lol! Do you need whiskey??!!

Paul Simmonds—Blank Box Design and Print. I call, say I need a book cover. You're walking your dog. All you have is the name of the book and 'my' colours. It was as simple as that. You've recreated my mad ideas into images, consistently for all these years, and I love that I can proclaim your genius and say an official thank you in print, in public, because I'm not sure you know how integral you have been to all my business adventures. I should tell you more often! Maybe I should send some whiskey as a thank you?!

Simone Chierchini—Publisher. A man with such solid values, it was impossible for me not to work with you… because if ordinary people don't help each other, who else will?

Shari Tiegman—Performance Coach. Seen and heard, without needing to speak. Do I need to say any more?! Maverick kinfolk x

Advance Readers. Thank you for taking time out for my words. Some of your words that came back will be etched in my heart forever.

Kay and Marianna—The Make Up Spot. Because everyone needs a therapist, and mine just happen to be beauty therapists!

Aunty Jackie and Antie Patsy – it's a love thing xx

Maria. For catching me and reminding me who the fuck I am.

Those who we've lost. Thank you for your love. Thank you for your lessons.

Melenie

Jose

Kathleen

Mom

Pete

Neslie

Matthew

Vince

Uncle Jim

Grandad

Nana

The Glory of Being Ordinary
Book 2

Money
Can anyone make a Million?

by Dawn Willock

Don't spend money – circulate it.

I am an ordinary woman. I also like having money.

I looked to deconstruct my feelings about money. Why am I not embarrassed to speak about it? Why do I have less shame than others about it, but also, why I don't have more – or why I don't have less? Why are some of us richer than others? What are our consequences?

This book is not a "Get Rich Quick' or '5 Ways to Financial Wealth' scheme, but rather a set of questions we can explore and solutions we can contemplate. As with everything I do, my first strategy is mindset. Fix perspective, then apply the practical tactics.

The book is purposefully directed towards the word 'money' instead of describing it as 'wealth.' Wealth means many things, reaching far beyond money. I am reasonably irritated about how we pussy foot around it all. So, I will not insult anyone's intelligence by trying to con you into anything by prettying it up, using the word wealth. And I want to overcome the 'righteous' among us who must add alternative definitions to appease their beliefs. Instead, I will be upfront and clarify from the outset, even though we probably do have to explore other 'wealth' definitions – this narrative is, specifically, intentionally most deliberately written to talk to ordinary people and money.

Specifically, about having more money.
Intentionally, about having more money.

Deliberately, about me genuinely wanting ordinary people to have more money.

And why would I like that?

I am fed up with all the noise. As I move into middle age and make friends with my mortality, my contemplation moves me to reflect and consider the choices I make, the beliefs I hold and what impact that has had on how much money I have – or not have - and what difference that has upon life, happiness and the choices ordinary people have as a result. I am left yearning to inspire people to peek around a door of possibility around money and ponder with me, what it might be like to take advantage of money without feeling like they have sold their souls. Fundamentally, I would like us all to have more.

This book is for ordinary people, with whom I'd very much like to have a conversation about poverty and being rich.

Why am I writing this book?

Money is a big part of our lives, whether we like it or not. If we can nail having enough money to have choices without selling our souls, then that's a very sweet spot. I genuinely believe that anyone can have more money. That concept may be a little off beat for some. I want to have the opportunity to explain this, to explore the concept – to investigate why I see this as so AND to investigate why many don't see any truth whatsoever in the possibility that ANYONE can have more money.

I guess this is as much of a self-discovery book about money, alongside hopefully uplifting some other ordinary people who perhaps are interested enough, open enough and brave enough to come on a little investigative journey, into our minds, into our beliefs and our decisions around money. It is always a brave thing to question your own status quo.

I also wondered…

What if we played with this more purposefully? What if there was a collective community challenge, where it wasn't some 5-day freebie and a sales pitch at the end to buy a course or mastermind – what if we light-heartedly just asked ourselves a few questions, apply the word 'why' and 'why not' a little, to see if we changed that around a bit and if we could all have more money?

Just for the sheer fun of it!

I don't worship money. It often isn't my biggest motivator, and I know many who have far more than me. I have known poverty, and have known happiness without money – all said, I don't seem to fear money, or have any significant barrier to accepting it. And I love the choices that money offers.

As I move swiftly towards the age of retirement, I do know, I would like more. I have developed this momentum throughout my life, which is both a blessing and a curse. I have inherited the saleswoman and entrepreneurial skills of my mother, and the hard-working integrity of my father.

I am a product of my parents, their beliefs, and their patterns, then I have sprinkled my translation of that as a little bit of extra frosting. And yet, although I am in a very comfortable position now, I don't seem to have as much money as I would like – that needs questioning, quite quickly!

I have an abundant belief around money, however, I think what I have also developed this recipe of always relying on making it when I HAVE to, and because I am good at doing that, there also seems to be a pattern of requiring a little drama in order for me to pull my finger out! I have hit a bit of a realisation around that. I don't want the drama. I don't want the weight of having to react. Instead, I now want a bit more of a plan, where it is less reliant on the patterns I have developed over the years. I seek a little more solace around security.

Woven tightly into the fabric of our DNA, we know. We know when we have settled, or when we are avoiding some of the evidence around us. If you struggle with money, either having it or not having it, this indicates you have some questions to ask.

I know I have some questions to ask myself.

This story isn't my story, rather words about the way we make life hard for ourselves, usually wrapped up in a package that we want the easy route.

It's about resilience, self-worth, and courage. It is about the critical relationship we have around money and how beliefs impact every decision we make, and words which dare to challenge beliefs and break down barriers. It's my journey, but it's also everyone else's. We all have the same availability for life lessons. We all get the same opportunity to extract what's in our souls. We are all just ordinary people.

The irony is how unimportant a single person's journey really is, the insignificance of the details, because we live, we die, and the next generation moves forwards. Rinse and repeat.

I could easily apply self-sabotage and question what right I have to write a book about money. Surely only multi-millionaires get to speak on this. And therein is the point. They are extremely wealthy, and we are not! So, let's explore that together!

But I like to add a bit more of a twist. I set myself a challenge. It starts 1st January 2024. The challenge is to make an extra £1 million in the next year. I have a plan (ish) but first, I have to make sure my mind is truly on board. I have to explore my perspective, beliefs, patterns and habits. I need to look myself hard in the mirror, ask myself some hard questions and face those truths.

I am going to put myself in enormous vulnerability and publicly document how I get on, and ask that you all join in.

What do you reckon? Fancy giving it a go?

Scan the QR code, connect with me, and let's see what happens together!

The Ran Network
https://therannetwork.com

Printed in Great Britain
by Amazon

31141922R00088